M000190468

Allelujah!

Alan Bennett has been one of our leading dramatists since the success of *Beyond the Fringe* in the 1960s. His television series *Talking Heads* has become a modern-day classic, as have many of his works for stage including *Forty Years On*, *The Lady in the Van*, *A Question of Attribution*, *The Madness of George III* (together with the Oscar-nominated screenplay *The Madness of King George*) and an adaptation of Kenneth Grahame's *The Wind in the Willows*. At the National Theatre, London, *The History Boys* won numerous awards including *Evening Standard* and Critics' Circle awards for Best Play, an Olivier for Best New Play and the South Bank Award. On Broadway, *The History Boys* won five New York Drama Desk Awards, four Outer Critics' Circle Awards, a New York Drama Critics' Award, a New York Drama League Award and six Tonys. *The Habit of Art* opened at the National in 2009 and *People* in 2012, together with two short plays, *Hymn* and *Cocktail Sticks*.

His latest collection of prose, *Keeping On Keeping On*, was published in 2016. Of his two previous collections, *Writing Home* was a number-one bestseller and *Untold Stories* won the PEN/Ackerley Prize for autobiography, 2006. Bennett's *Six Poets, Hardy to Larkin: an Anthology*, was published in 2014. His fiction includes *The Uncommon Reader* and *Smut: Two Unseemly Stories*.

by the same author

PLAYS ONE
(*Forty Years On, Getting On, Habeas Corpus, Enjoy*)

PLAYS TWO
(*Kafka's Dick, The Insurance Man, The Old Country,
An Englishman Abroad, A Question of Attribution*)

THE LADY IN THE VAN
OFFICE SUITE
THE MADNESS OF GEORGE III
THE WIND IN THE WILLOWS
THE HISTORY BOYS
THE HABIT OF ART
PEOPLE
HYMN *and* COCKTAIL STICKS

television plays

ME, I'M AFRAID OF VIRGINIA WOOLF
(*A Day Out, Sunset Across the Bay, A Visit from Miss Prothero,
Me, I'm Afraid of Virginia Woolf, Green Forms, The Old Crowd,
Afternoon Off*)

ROLLING HOME
(*One Fine Day, All Day on the Sands, Our Winnie,
Rolling Home, Marks, Say Something Happened, Intensive Care*)

TALKING HEADS

screenplays

A PRIVATE FUNCTION
(*The Old Crowd, A Private Function, Prick Up Your Ears,
102 Boulevard Haussmann, The Madness of King George*)

THE HISTORY BOYS: THE FILM

autobiography

THE LADY IN THE VAN
WRITING HOME
UNTOLD STORIES
A LIFE LIKE OTHER PEOPLE'S

fiction

THREE STORIES
(*The Laying on of Hands, The Clothes They Stood Up In,
Father! Father! Burning Bright*)

THE UNCOMMON READER
SMUT: TWO UNSEEMLY STORIES

ALAN BENNETT

Allelujah!

with an introduction by the author

FABER & FABER

This edition first published in 2018
by Faber and Faber Limited
74–77 Great Russell Street
London WC1B 3DA

Typeset by Country Setting, Kingsdown, Kent CT14 8ES
Printed in England by CPI Bookmarque, Croydon, Surrey

© Forelake Ltd, 2018

The right of Alan Bennett to be identified as author
of this work has been asserted in accordance with Section 77
of the Copyright, Designs and Patents Act 1988

'Ten Types of Hospital Visitor' © Charles Causley,
from *Collected Poems 1951-2000* (Macmillan), reproduced
by permission of David Higham Associates Limited

All rights whatsoever in this work, amateur or professional, are
strictly reserved. Applications for permission for any use whatsoever
including performance rights must be made in advance, prior to
any such proposed use, to United Agents, 12–26 Lexington Street,
London W1F 0LE. No performance may be given unless a licence
has first been obtained.

This book is sold subject to the condition that it shall not,
by way of trade or otherwise, be lent, resold, hired out
or otherwise circulated without the publisher's prior consent
in any form of binding or cover other than that in which
it is published and without a similar condition including
this condition being imposed on the subsequent purchaser

A CIP record for this book is available from the British Library

ISBN
pbk 978-0-571-34985-2
hbk 978-0-571-35064-3
limited edn 978-0-571-35065-0

2 4 6 8 10 9 7 5 3 1

Acknowledgements

Allelujah! has turned out to be a much bigger proposition than I'd imagined when I'd finished writing it. I blithely included a possible choir without indicating how many singers there were or what or where they should sing. My only stipulation was that it shouldn't include the geriatric Horst Wessel 'I am h-a-p-p-y'. Nicholas Hytner, to whom after twenty-eight years of working together I am almost routinely indebted, saw more possibilities in the play than I had, seizing on my brief stage directions to make the choir a staple feature of the production and with dance besides. This brought in my friend and long-term collaborator George Fenton who has arranged the music and, in charge of the (to me, wonderful) dancing, Arlene Phillips. The pair of them have coaxed out of the cast music and movement of which they may have thought themselves incapable. I hope they have found the experience enjoyable; neither singer nor dancer myself, I have often envied them. We have had much help and encouragement from our medical advisor Jonathan Sheldon and also from the staff of various hospitals, particularly Leeds General Infirmary, Killingbeck Hospital in Leeds and St Mary's, Paddington.

In his opening talk to the cast, Nicholas Hytner said, 'We may not get it right but we will get it real.' I'd like to thank everyone who has helped in that process.

Introduction

I have been writing plays (slightly to my surprise) for fifty years and more and it is a bit late in the day to confess that I tend to write before I do the research. Otherwise, knowing myself, I'm likely to get too interested not to say bogged down in the facts and so never get round to the play itself.

I first realised this in the 1960s when I was just beginning as a writer, putting together sketches for the Saturday night TV shows that came after *That Was the Week that Was*. I knew nothing about television and not much more about sketch writing and so made the mistake of over-researching a topic in order to pull out facts that the audience didn't know. This may have been informative but it wasn't always funny and I learned early on that in order to interest and amuse an audience one needed to know more than they did but not much more. Ever since I've tended to write first and ask questions afterwards. One of the many reasons why I'm happily paired with Nicholas Hytner is that he is of a more literal cast of mind and readily researches the necessary background, querying many of my fanciful notions before putting them to rights. Notably in this play he saw straightaway that in my original draft I was confusing a geriatric ward with a care home and that the difference must be made plain.

I did have some excuse. In theory a geriatric ward is confined to patients who need medical attention because they are ill. They may be ill because they are elderly but age alone does not qualify them for the geriatric ward. It does qualify them for a care home which is for the elderly who don't require medical attention but do need round-the-clock care. That the difference is not always obvious is because a patient on a geriatric ward who has recovered can't always be discharged since there is nowhere to discharge him or her to . . . no relative willing or able to have them, no vacancy in a care home that would, not to mention the possible expense. So they stay put in the geriatric ward and become bed-blockers and in the process the geriatric ward becomes more like a care home than the hospital would like.

Seldom in hospital myself until I was in my sixties such experience as I've had has found its way into the play. When I was first hospitalised as a young man nurses were more likely to be disciplinarians than they are today. Beds were squared off and kept in apple-pie order pending the awed arrival of the consultant with his respectful train of underlings. Nowadays nurses have been robbed of their starch and doctors of their white coats and consultants have been known actually to sit on a patient's bed, all of them casualties of deference and its decline.

The kindest nurse I ever came across wasn't a nurse at all. Having been operated on for bowel cancer in 1997 I'd been admitted a few months later to the old Middlesex Hospital off Goodge Street with acute pains in my stomach which were unsurprisingly thought to be a recurrence. Thankfully this proved not to be the case, the culprit an abscess on what remained of my appendix. This had to be drained via a tube introduced through the wall of the stomach. Assuming this would be done under Valium (a drug I've always found delightful), I was unworried and indeed the procedure seemed quite casual, taking place in a curtained alcove off quite a busy corridor in the basement. The doctor with a medical student in attendance busied himself with his preparations which included positioning the screen so that he could follow the tube tracing the source of the infection. It was only when I felt a winding blow to my stomach that I realised there was going to be no anaesthetic and not even a painkiller.

As this scalding snake felt its way round my gut I was in agony, though the doctor and the student, both intent on their screen, seemed indifferent to my cries of pain. At this moment a young man came down the corridor, not a doctor certainly and not, I think, a nurse, but just a theatre orderly in hospital greens. Sizing up the situation, unasked he stopped and took my hand. It can only have been a minute or two before the abscess was found and a drain introduced but it was long enough for me to think that this uncalled-for gesture was perhaps the kindest thing anyone had ever done for me. As the drain began to produce pus in gratifying quantities the young man patted my arm and went on his way.

It's at this point that life connects with art and the story becomes relevant, as afterwards the doctor made the student examine my emaciated stomach to see if he could find the slight pulse which would be an indication of peristalsis, the automatic muscular contractions by which the contents of the alimentary canal are propelled through the body. It's the procedure which Dr Valentine in the play explains to Colman as a (slightly far-fetched) metaphor for the slow and steady working of the hospital itself. Back on the ward I tried to find out who was my Samaritan but without success, though I was later told that he had become a doctor himself. I hope so.

In one respect the play makes no attempt at realism. Though mitigated these days by the laptop any ward is still dominated by the television screen, chattering away and the background to pain, sorrow and even death. In our hospital I imagine the TV has been banished to a so-called quiet room though in a proper hospital this would probably be unacceptable.

The absence of television is matched by the non-presence of visitors. Though patients on a geriatric ward are more likely to have visitors than the inmates of a care home, a geriatric ward is hardly a magnet for friends and family –

friends mostly dead and family getting on with their lives. It's more likely to be duty than affection that brings company to an old person's bedside. And once there what to say as one sits by the bed, these wearisome visits less like meetings than periods of sentry duty with the visitor on the look-out for some glimmer of hope or sense. The whole scenario is definitively dealt with in Charles Causley's poem, 'Ten Types of Hospital Visitor', which is quoted in the play.

One of the main characters in the play is Salter, the chairman of the Hospital Trust. He is much in evidence, talking to the nurses, welcoming new arrivals, very much – and perhaps implausibly for a chairman – hands on. My doubts about Salter's over-eager involvement were stilled when the director and the designer, Bob Crowley, visited several hospitals in the interest of authenticity and several nurses reassured them that cameras were always a magnet and, 'If there's filming going on, the chairman's never away.'

Writing a play I have never tried to hide the sound of my own voice. It hasn't always been where an audience or a critic has thought to find it and certainly not always in the mouth of the leading character. It's often a divided voice or a dissenting one; two things (at least) are being said and I am not always sure which one I agree with. But that is one reason why I write plays: one can speak with a divided voice. In *Allelujah!* it means that I have some sympathy with Salter and with Nurse Gilchrist, neither of whom is entirely sympathetic. I subscribe to Chekhov's dictum that, 'It is the writer's business not to accuse and not to prosecute but to champion the guilty once they are condemned and suffer punishment.'

Staged as it is in my eighty-fourth year the play could be taken as a would-be apotheosis though I hope not. It does include occasional jokes that have been with me half my writing life without (perhaps understandably) ever finding a place. Was it at Pontefract Barracks during my basic training in the infantry in 1952 or a few years later in the Ministry of Pensions hospital in Leeds that I heard another soldier make the sauce bottle remark? Now, after sixty years, Joe has it to say. Or I hope he does. That depends if it survives the rehearsals which at the time of writing have not yet started. One of Nicholas Hytner's skills is as a surgeon, slicing away such inessentials – a cosmetic surgeon perhaps, doing lipectomies but never trespassing into the vitals. There will be cuts and alterations so that the script one ends up with is a bit of a bumpy field, the mounds and hollows reminiscent of a deserted village – Wharram Percy it would be, the famous deserted village in North Yorkshire. With ditches marking the site of lost dialogue and occasional tracks that lead nowhere, for me all my plays have a touch of Wharram Percy.

Plays as I first submit them to Nicholas Hytner are generally quite loose-fitting garments which can then be tailored to his (and sometimes the cast's) strengths and requirements. Also doing the tailoring in *Allelujah!* is George Fenton who has arranged the music and whom I've known all my working life as he began his career as a young actor in my first play *Forty Years On.*

I have always thought there is an element of unsought prophecy in plays: write it and it happens. With this play it's been almost embarrassing. Lest I be thought to be trailing behind the facts I should say that Valentine's trouble over his visa was written months before the Windrush business. I had originally intended Valentine to be an older doctor, brought out of retirement by the hospital because of shortage of staff. In which case to refuse him a visa would have seemed more shocking, though no more so than the treatment meted out to the long-established immigrants who were so callously singled out.

If not quite a platform, a play is certainly a plinth, a small eminence from which to address the world, hold forth about one's concerns or the concerns of one's characters. But not to preach. That is forbidden, though the fact that I always like it when a character steps out of the play and addresses the audience is evidence that I am a thwarted preacher with no other way than this to broadcast my paltry epiphanies. I never like feeling boxed-in by the fourth wall. In this play, though, that problem is to some extent sidestepped as the characters can within the play still address the roving camera, though some more furtively than others. It's only in the last few minutes that Valentine gets to speak unmediated to the audience, by which time he has earned the right . . . and maybe that's why he smiles.

Alan Bennett
May 2018

Allelujah! was first performed at the Bridge Theatre, London, on 11 July 2018. The cast, in alphabetical order, was as follows:

PATIENTS

Molly Jacqueline Chan
Mrs Maudsley Jacqueline Clarke
Mavis Patricia England
Mary Julia Foster
Arthur Colin Haigh
Renee Anna Lindup
Neville Louis Mahoney
Joe Jeff Rawle
Cora Cleo Sylvestre
Lucille Gwen Taylor
Hazel Sue Wallace
Ambrose Simon Williams

STAFF

Dr Valentine Sacha Dhawan
Sister Gilchrist Deborah Findlay
Salter Peter Forbes
Ramesh Manish Gandhi
Gerald Richie Hart
Nurse Pinkney Nicola Hughes
Fletcher Gary Wood

VISITORS

Colin Samuel Barnett
Alex Sam Bond

Mrs Earnshaw Rosie Ede
Cliff Nadine Higgin
Andy David Moorst
Mr Earnshaw Duncan Wisbey

Other parts played by members of the company

Director Nicholas Hytner
Designer Bob Crowley
Choreographer Arlene Phillips
Music George Fenton
Lighting Designer Natasha Chivers
Sound Designer Mike Walker
Assistant Director Sean Linnen
Associate Designer Jaimie Todd
Assistant Choreographer Richard Roe
Music Director Richie Hart
Casting Director Toby Whale
*Costume Superviso*r Lynette Mauro
Hair, Wigs and Make-up Campbell Young Associates
Props Supervisors Marcus Hall Props

Characters

Fletcher
a junior doctor

Gerald
physiotherapist

VISITORS

Colin Colman
Joe's son, management consultant

Mrs Earnshaw

Mr Earnshaw

Andy
work experience

Alex
documentary director

Cliff
cameraman

Voice

Nurses, Healthcare Assistants, Social Workers etc.

Musical Numbers

'Yours'
(music Gonzalo Roig, lyrics Albert Gamse
and Jack Sherr)

'You Made Me Love You (I Didn't Want to Do It)
(music James V. Monaco, lyrics Joseph McCarthy)

'A, You're Adorable'
(music Sid Lippmann, lyrics Buddy Kaye and Fred Wise,
arranged by George Fenton)

'Love and Marriage'
(music Jimmy Van Heusen, lyrics Sammy Cahn,
arranged by Nelson Riddle, sung by Frank Sinatra)

'Good Morning'
(music Nacio Herb Brown, lyrics Arthur Freed,
arranged by George Fenton)

'Blow the Wind Southerly'
(traditional, arranged by George Fenton)

'Good Golly, Miss Molly
(music and lyrics John Marascalco and
Robert "Bumps" Blackwell, sung by Little Richard)

'On the Sunny Side of the Street'
(music Jimmy McHugh, lyrics Dorothy Fields,
arranged by George Fenton)

'I Can Give You the Starlight'
(music and lyrics Ivor Novello,
arranged by George Fenton, sung by Gary Wood)

'Congratulations'
(music and lyrics Bill Martin and Phil Coulter,
arranged by George Fenton)

'Side by Side'
(music and lyrics Harry M. Woods,
arranged by George Fenton)

'Get Happy'
(music Harold Arlen, lyrics Ted Koehler,
arranged by George Fenton)

ALLELUJAH!

And thou most kind and gentle death,
Waiting to hush our latest breath.
O praise him! Alleluia!

Part One

A provincial hospital. Stage pretty bare.

MUSIC: 'Yours' (Vera Lynn).

An old lady in a wheelchair, very decrepit but with a good voice, sings, accompanied on a cracked hospital piano, as behind her comes up a panorama of a Northern city – Morley, say, or Wakefield.
  A doctor at the side of the stage – Asian, thirty-five to forty – observes the old lady, Mrs Maudsley.

Mrs Maudsley It was my house.

  Sister Gilchrist now appears, tidies up the old lady and takes her off.

Dr Valentine Those with dementia can sometimes sing even when they cannot talk.

Gilchrist What is there to sing about?

Valentine They can even dance.

Mrs Maudsley It was my house.

Pinkney Dr Valentine. You're wanted on the ward.

  Valentine leaves as a youngish man, aged around thirty – Colin Colman – cycles into view, Lycra-clad and on a posh racing bike. Mobile in ear, he talks and rides without holding the handlebars.

Colin I'm here. Home. Yeah. What?

  He consults his wrist.

A hundred and ninety-eight miles.

No, coming up to it now.

In fact, some twat in an ambulance has just cut me up.

I *am* hi-vis. Lycra from head to toe – you could see me from the fucking moon.

Sorry. It's just being back.

Oh, much as ever. The town. The hospital. And beyond the hospital, the distant moors.

No, not Muslims, you dick, *moors*. Heather, gorse. Jesus. No further word from on high? The Minister not minded to make up his mind yet? No?

Anyway, this is a private visit.

My dad, George. My ailing father, patient in the said threatened hospital.

Love? Sure, I'll give it him, George. Not that he's ever wanted mine.

Anyway. (*About to ring off, he hears singing from the hospital.*) Hear that, George? The ancestral anthems of the North.

Colin pauses before cycling off down the hill at the back of the stage.

In the hospital, a line of old people file on, singing 'Yours', and sit in a row of armchairs, shepherded by two nurses: Gilchrist and Pinkney. Gerald, the ward physio, is at the keyboards. When not playing for them, he is in constant attendance, working on their mobility. Valentine also present.

A two-person camera crew film them coming on.

The nurses arrange them into position, with Gilchrist occasionally inspecting the skirt of one of the women to check they haven't wet themselves and feeling the trousers of the men similarly.

Lucille Mr Jessop's gone.

Hazel Has he?

Lucille Went in the night, the way people do. Mind you, he was very obese.

Pinkney We shall miss him in the choir because he was a bass.

Gilchrist Maybe he was a bass because he was obese.

Pinkney One day, Sister Gilchrist, you'll learn to take this choir seriously.

Possibly there is a withered balloon somewhere, which Valentine retrieves. Or a streamer reading: 'Save the Beth'. As the old people settle, the camera is positioned for their interview. Alex is the director, Cliff camera and sound.

Alex Hello, boys and girls. What I thought we might do is if you told me your name and a bit about yourself.

Molly bangs a tin tray.

Gilchrist Molly. Give me your tray, there's a good girl.

Molly clutches the tray and shakes her head.

Well, hug it, love. Don't bang it.

Pinkney Don't look at the camera, Neville, don't look. The camera is not here.

Neville I can see it.

Pinkney It's not here.

Alex Right. Who's first? What about you?

Lucille My father had a chain of confectioners.

Pinkney Say your name, Lucille.

Lucille Lucille. It's French.

Alex Are you French?

Lucille No. I'm from Morley.

Alex And why are you here?

Lucille Well, because I'm old.

Mavis We're all old. What's the matter with you besides?

Lucille I keep having these dizzy dos. By rights I should be a private patient.

Mavis What does it matter? Dead, we'll all be the same.

Ambrose Don't you believe it. Heaven'll be the same as Heathrow. There'll be a VIP Lounge.

Alex Now a man perhaps.

Joe I'm not so well either. My chest sounds like a sack of wet gravel. I'm on tablets.

Neville We're all on tablets.

Joe Did anybody ask you?

Neville Yes. He did.

Joe I was a miner and with the mining I got a bad chest. Black lung. That was before Mrs Thatcher put paid to the mines.

Lucille Don't start.

Hazel Did your father do vanilla slices?

Lucille I can't remember.

Hazel Not much of a confectioner if he didn't do vanilla slices. They think I've got an ulcer.

Joe It's all them vanilla slices.

What about you, Mr . . . ?

Ambrose Hammersley. Ambrose Hammersley.

Alex What were you in life?

Ambrose In life, as you put it, I was a schoolmaster. Now in a wheelchair due to osteo-arthritis, and a fall. Legs gone.

6

Hazel I've got that a bit, too, arthritis. He's lovely. We're engaged.

Ambrose Take no notice. The lady is confused.

Hazel I push him sometimes.

Ambrose Bugger off.

Lucille Language!

Ambrose Don't 'language' me. I taught language.

Lucille You didn't teach that.

Alex Next?

Gilchrist You, Neville.

Neville No.

Gilchrist He's a bit shy, aren't you, Neville?

Neville No. Only I have that thing where you go up and down.

Joe Sex?

Gilchrist Bi-polar.

Neville I've been in and out of hospital all my life.

Gilchrist So who does that leave? Mavis?

Mavis (*who is still doing her make-up*) I'm still whitening the sepulchre.

Gilchrist Cora?

Cora Can I do mine later? That mince we had keeps rifting up. I feel a bit wanny.

Pinkney I'll get you a tablet, love.

Mavis I'm ready for my close-up.

Lucille Look out! She's got her eyelashes on.

Gilchrist This is Mavis. Who was a dancer.

Alex Whereabouts?

Mavis I travelled the world.

Lucille Gateshead mainly.

Pinkney Fratch, fratch, fratch. Now stop it, the pair of you. Cora, are you sure there's nothing you want to say?

Cora Well, the level of my Lucozade keeps going down. I think one of these is supping it.

Lucille Mavis. Tell the camera what you're in with.

Mavis I don't remember.

Lucille Piles. Haemorrhoids.

Mavis It never is. They don't know what I've got. I'm under observation.

Pinkney But we're all of us happy, aren't we?

Ambrose Pass.

Pinkney And where is it we don't want to go?

Hazel The lavatory?

Pinkney We don't want to go to Tadcaster.

Joe Why? It's got a grand brewery.

Cliff (*to Valentine*) Maybe you should explain.

Valentine Should the Beth have to close, the geriatric wards would all be transferred to a custom-built facility at Tadcaster.

Pinkney And we don't want that, do we?

Hazel Don't we? Why?

Pinkney So. All together now. Save the Beth!

All Save the Beth!

Gerald plays.

MUSIC: 'You Made Me Love You'.

The old people sing from song sheets. A few seconds into the number, the music transforms, the hospital dissolves, and the old people rise from their chairs, throw their sticks away, and dance as if young again.
By the end of the number, they are old again, in their chairs.
Valentine takes Mary's hand. He often, when talking to his patients, strokes their arm – not offensively, but noticeably. As the old people leave:

Valentine Oh Mary, they missed you out.

Mary Don't let on. I don't mind. I'm not used to saying much through working in a library. And everyone else has got so much off. No.

Valentine Are you sure?

Mary I'm sure.

As Mary follows the rest of them offstage, Valentine turns to the camera crew.

Valentine Bed?

Alex Sure.

Valentine now pushes an empty bed frame on to the stage. He is about to address the camera when there is a call for his services.

Valentine This is what the hospital is about.

His pager goes off.

(*For the benefit of the camera.*) Sorry! I'm wanted.

At which point, Salter comes on, plainly relishing the camera. A smooth, urbane, well set-up figure who condescends to Valentine. He is in high spirits.

Salter No problem, Dr Valentine. I'll take over.

A bed. The secret of our success.

Something to die for. Something to die in, too, of course, but, always in short supply, what makes a good hospital is an available bed. It's what I'm confident will make the Minister come down in our favour. Because our figures are good. Very good. And one way or another, we always manage to find a bed.

Then Colin cycles through.

Salter No cycling in the hospital precincts! Young man! (*Sweetly. It is on camera after all.*) No cycling! Where was I?

Cliff The bed.

A lad of about seventeen comes on, pushing an empty wheelchair.

Andy William Wordsworth?

Salter shakes his head and Andy retreats, but doesn't go off.

Salter A bed matters. Doctors make a difference, of course, but this is what counts. Is there a bed?

Andy Doctor. Doctor.

Salter doesn't let him speak.

Salter William Wordsworth is Joan Collins. Keep up! (*And points a finger in the direction.*)

Andy Got you.

Salter (*calling after him*) And I am not a doctor. I am a lot of things but I am not a doctor.

Andy (*to himself, going off*) Well you've got glasses on.

Salter (*to the camera*) That young man, possibly born in this hospital because the Beth is nothing if not local, with its own maternity facility at one end of the scale and its geriatric wards at the other. Both ends of life catered for. Beth short for Bethlehem, so called when it was founded in the eighteenth century because, like the inn, nobody was turned away. Not quite the case today, but it is still what we want to do. And if we are allowed to. Our fate now hangs in the balance. At best – best! – there is a move to hive off our geriatric wards and move them to Tadcaster. At worst to shut down the hospital altogether. Is this much-loved establishment to close? We have had the Inquiry. We await the outcome. But we must keep up the pressure. Save the Beth!

Valentine has returned.

Alex Cut. Lovely.

Valentine Did you want to be a doctor?

Salter (*off-camera now*) Oh yes. I wanted to be a physician . . . Grave, judicious, reassuring. Doctors these days tend to come in shirtsleeves and pullover. Which is a pity. (*For the camera.*) Perhaps you should ask me what my function is.

Alex Go ahead.

Valentine What is your function Mr Salter, if you're not a doctor?

Salter For my sins I am the chairman of the Hospital Trust, though as many viewers will know, I've been a lot of other things besides, including Lord Mayor (twice!). Chairman is a grand title but I hope not a remote one and I'm often around – indeed patients have been known to wake up from the anaesthetic to find the sometime

Lord Mayor pushing their bed back to the ward and thinking perhaps they've died and gone to heaven.

Valentine's pager goes off and he leaves once again.

(*Off-camera.*) This (*i.e. Valentine's absence*) gives me a chance to say that I'm not sure how much you want to see of Valentine. Sister Gilchrist may be a better tip. He says he chose geriatrics because he likes old people – but nobody likes old people. Old people don't like old people (though don't put that in). A serious fellow, he's trying to write a book, as doctors tend to do (as if they haven't got enough on their plates). And don't let him start talking to you about medicine. (*He mimes a yawn.*)

Ah, Valentine!

Valentine ushers in a middle-aged couple, and Mrs Earnshaw's mother, Mrs Maudsley, who is in a wheelchair, and whom we have seen at the start, singing. Gilchrist and Pinkney in attendance.

I'll take this, Doctor.

Gilchrist Are you sure? They're filming it.

Salter Are they? Oh – (*Mock surprise.*) Still, it keeps my hand in.

Now, who're we admitting? (*He takes her file.*) Mrs Earnshaw.

Valentine No. Mrs Maudsley.

Suddenly there is a disturbance.

Ramesh Coming through!

A young doctor – Ramesh – rushes through, pushing a patient in a wheelchair, possibly with a nurse in tow, holding up the drip.

Salter makes no comment on this incursion, but just gives a wide, inclusive smile.

Salter (*to Valentine*) Have they been told about the camera?

Valentine nods.

(*Mouthing.*) Don't look at the camera.
Now, tell me about mother. (*Stifling a yawn.*) I'm interested. Had a fall. Got confused. We've managed to find her a bed on Shirley Bassey.
They are fortunate, are they not, Valentine, that there is still a ward for the bed to go on.
Now, Mrs Earnshaw.

Mrs Earnshaw No. I'm Mrs Earnshaw. Mother is Mrs Maudsley.

Mr Earnshaw And I'm Mr Earnshaw.

Salter (*very loudly*) Hello!

Mrs Maudsley It was my house.

She begins to cry, this tempting the camera out.
Salter ignores Mrs Maudsley as the camera laps up the tears

Earnshaw She's confused.

Salter Quite so.

Mrs Earnshaw And she's got gallstones.

Salter Valentine?

Valentine Some routine questions. Is mother compos mentis? All there?

Mrs Earnshaw Oh yes. Catch her on a good day and she's as bright as a button.

Mrs Maudsley It was my house.

Valentine Is she mobile at all?

Earnshaw When it suits her.

Gilchrist Is she continent?

Mrs Earnshaw Oh yes.

Earnshaw rolls his eyes.

Salter That's good news.

Gilchrist We have better things to do than empty bedpans.

Valentine Though needs must.

Salter Of course. Of course.

Valentine Appetite?

Earnshaw She eats like a navvy.

Salter At the Beth, we like patients to join in. Is Mrs Maudsley social at all?

Mrs Earnshaw Oh yes. Life and soul of the party. Aren't you, Mother? Life and soul of the party.

Mrs Maudsley Mine. They took it.

Valentine Religion?

Mrs Maudsley Thieves.

Mrs Earnshaw She was C of E but with all these vicars being had up she went over to atheism.

Pinkney Do you sing at all?

Mrs Earnshaw Sing? Sing? This is the Pudsey Nightingale. Sing, Mother

Earnshaw Oh hell.

Mrs Maudsley sings a little.

MUSIC: 'I Can Give You the Starlight' (Ivor Novello).

Pinkney We love singing. We're having a concert next week for Sister Gilchrist. You can be our guest artist.

Salter (*for the camera's benefit*) And away she goes, about to take her place in the therapeutic community.

Pinkney wheels her away.
   Salter indicates the interview is at an end and Mrs Earnshaw gets up. Earnshaw doesn't.
   The following is out of earshot of the camera.

Earnshaw What's the survival rate?

Salter I'm sorry?

Earnshaw How long do they last?

Salter Well . . . that depends. This is a geriatric facility, after all . . .

Mrs Earnshaw He means generally speaking.

Earnshaw No, I don't.
   Six years ago she made over the house.

Mrs Earnshaw Only because she wanted to.

Earnshaw In order to avoid estate duty.

Mrs Earnshaw Perfectly legally. The Queen Mother did it.

Earnshaw She put the house in our name and come September it will be ours free of tax . . .

Salter I'm familiar with the arrangement.

Earnshaw I told you. Everybody does it. Only what I want is reassurance that she's going to last those three months.

Salter This is a hospital. We make people . . . last . . . as long as possible. And once they've dealt with the gallstones she may be out quite soon.

Mr Earnshaw (*as they are going out*) I don't think it is gallstones.

Mrs Earnshaw No, I don't either. I think it's you.

Salter (*also going out but for the benefit of the camera*)
Salt of the earth!

Salter takes them out, leaving Valentine onstage, alone, but with the camera.

Valentine Ready? Now?

Cliff (*camera*) Coast clear.

Valentine An extract from my book:
If all property is theft no one in here has any property.
Unwaged, unpensioned, disendowed of their homes, all
too often they are disendowed of the faculties that went
with them. Loss of things means loss of bearings. So now,
unanchored, they begin to drift, clinging to their lockers
like Ahab to his coffin.

Cliff gives Valentine the thumbs up and withdraws.
    *Colin lazily cycles through as Gilchrist is taking care
of Mrs Maudsley.*

Gilchrist Don't let them catch you in here with that
thing.

Colin Why? What'll they do?

Gilchrist Fine you, probably, same as they do in the car
park. They're demons. Are you looking for somebody?

Colin Dusty Springfield.

Gilchrist In person?

Colin Mr Colman.

Gilchrist Joe?

Colin You know him?

Gilchrist He's not so good at the moment.

Colin They phoned. That's why I'm here.

Gilchrist Are you the son? The one who knows the Prime Minister?

Colin I don't know the Prime Minister. That's just my dad. Though I am attached to the Department of Health.

Gilchrist More than we are.
  'Attached'. Joke.

Colin Yes. Ha ha.

Gilchrist Anyway, I'll be giving him a bath shortly. You're welcome to come.

Colin When you've finished.

Gilchrist We'll be in Fatima Whitbread.

The old people are gathered. Pinkney and Gerald take them through a number.

MUSIC: 'A, You're Adorable'.

Gerald goes to the hand sanitiser to ready himself for physio.

Lucille Where are you going, Mavis?

Mavis Gerald's going to do my back.

Lucille He never is. He's doing my leg.

Gilchrist Well, you're both wrong because he's doing my neck.

Lucille You're not a patient. That's incestuous.

Gilchrist It's a perk of the job. One of the few.

Lucille You want reporting, you. You shouldn't be doing that, Gerald.

Gerald Listen, I don't mind who I do. I'm anybody's.

Much whooping.

Hazel Did you like that?

Ambrose (*who as always has his earphones on*) Did I like what?

Hazel Us, singing.

Ambrose I didn't hear it.

Hazel I was singing it for you.

Ambrose I wouldn't bother.

Hazel You wouldn't say that if I was Dorothy Squires.

Ambrose On the contrary, I would say it if you were Kiri-Te-Fucking-Kanawa.

Hazel maybe weeps.

Do you know what that is, Hazel?

Hazel Yes, disgusting.

Ambrose It's also a grammatical construction called tmesis. Abso-bloody-lutely would be another example.

Valentine has come in.

You're privileged. Apart from me, Hazel, you are probably the only person in what was once the West Riding of Yorkshire who knows what tmesis is.

Hazel (*faintly*) Hurray.

Valentine I'll push him back, Hazel.

Pinkney Hazel?

He takes Hazel off.

Valentine You sound on good form.

Ambrose Yes. Ebbing. But still flowing Are you wanting to pick my brains again?

Valentine Do you mind?

18

Ambrose Nobody else thinks I have a brain to pick.

Valentine An enclitic?

Ambrose Fish 'n' chips. Rock 'n' roll. It's a connective. A shortened version of 'and'. Hairdressers like them for some reason. 'Cut 'n' dry', 'Curl up 'n' dye'.

Valentine And the other one was?

Ambrose Tmesis. Look it up.

Valentine I shall.

Ambrose This test. What is it?

Valentine Nothing. Just a proficiency test. Use of English, that sort of thing.

Ambrose By the hospital?

Valentine Possibly. It may never happen. People get hauled in now and again so it's as well to be prepared. I'm just hoping they may've forgotten me. It's not a problem.

Ambrose Oh, incidentally, one of my old pupils has promised to look me up . . .

Valentine I know. Don't worry. I'll alert them at Reception.

He is pushing Ambrose off.

Mr Jessop died this morning.

Ambrose That's rather rude.

Valentine Why?

Ambrose Didn't he realise there's a queue?

As they leave, Andy pushes on Joe in a wheelchair.

Andy There you are.

Joe And? Is that it?

Andy This is Fatima Whitbread. Somebody's supposed to come and wash you.

Joe Not you?

Andy No fear. I'm just work experience.

Joe Yesterday's lad had a cig. He passed the time of day. Gave me a drag.

Andy It's no smoking.

Joe So? Live a little. Your mind's not on this.

Andy On what?

Joe Experiencing work.

Andy It's boring.

Joe Well, that's one lesson you've learned. Work is boring. Tell me about your life.

Andy I'm young. I haven't had one yet.

Joe Well, you see, now that you bring it up, I have. I've met several members of the Royal Family for a start. Only the lower levels, I admit. The ones that are in the background when they're all on the balcony. And on one never-to-be-forgotten occasion, in Batley of all places, I opened the door for Michael Parkinson, who thanked me personally.

Have you had sexual intercourse?

Andy Yeah. Loads of times.

Joe What do you reckon to it?

Andy It's alright.

Joe So do you want to feel my foot?

Andy Your foot? It wouldn't be top of my list.

Joe Not in a sexual way. Clinically. I've no feeling in it and I have to keep checking it's not returned. The lad yesterday was gearing up to do it, only then he had a call on his mobile.

Andy I bet he did.

Joe You could wear rubber gloves. In fact, I'd prefer it if you did.

Andy Listen. I couldn't feel your foot even if I wanted to. Health and Safety.
   Talking of which, can you sign this?

He gives Joe a form.

You have to sign to say I've been satisfactory. I have to have your signature or I can't go up to the next level.

Joe Well you haven't been, have you? Satisfactory.

Andy Just sign the fucker.

Joe 'Did the trainee attend to the requirements of the patient?' No, you bloody didn't.
   On a scale of one to five. Excellent. Good. Average. Poor. Poooor. I'm an unsatisfied customer. And we're all customers now.

Gilchrist comes in with her trolley. A Healthcare Assistant helps her transfer Joe from his chair to a bed.

(*To Gilchrist.*) That's not me, that mark. I don't leave marks on the floor. Or anywhere else. It'll be a woman made that mark. Else a kiddy. I don't leave marks. When I've been in a place, there's no evidence I've ever been there. I want it writing down. I don't want it on my slate.

Andy I can't see no mark.

Joe Because you're not a professional. Someone with qualifications.

Talking of which, I'm one of the aristocracy here. I can wipe my own bottom. Can't I?

Gilchrist You can. Good morning, Joe.

Joe Don't 'good morning' me.

Gilchrist is preparing the washing things when Colin comes in, still wheeling the bike.

Colin Hello, Dad.

Joe I'm not your dad.
You? My son? Got up like that? Come on.

Colin So who am I?

Joe That's your problem. Somebody they've sent round. Some joker. They must think I'm barmy.

Gilchrist Not good today, I'm afraid. He's got an infection.

Joe I never have.

Gilchrist How would you know?

Andy Nice bike.

Colin Do you want a go?

Andy gets on the bike.

Joe My son works in London and he wasn't a bit like you.

Andy Hey, look: 'No cycling in the hospital precincts'.

Joe Not to put too fine a point on it, you look like a nancy.

Colin So is that a problem?

Joe Who for? Not for me. It might be a problem for you. Carry on claiming you're my son and looking like that and I'd belt you.

Gilchrist He's having a bad day.

Colin Dad, I'm your son

Gilchrist pulls a screen round the bed.

Gilchrist I'm going to take your trousers off.

Joe Of course you are. That's what your sort always does.

Andy I'll go wait outside.

He goes to the other side of the screen.

Gilchrist What are you? Work experience? Well, this is work. This is experience.

Andy I don't want to see his willy.

Gilchrist Nor do I, particularly.

Joe No danger. These days it's swelling the ranks of the unemployed.

Gilchrist You going to be a nurse?

Andy No fear. Computers.
I've given him my form but he won't sign it.

Gilchrist It's not important.

Andy I thought forms were important.

Joe They were important in the pit. Checking who'd come up and who hadn't – that was important. That's something else you've learned.

Gilchrist continues the bed bath.

Gilchrist Could you help me?

Colin is plainly reluctant and turns his head away so he doesn't see his dad's nakedness. Joe doesn't like it either, and he struggles.

Joe No, no. Get off me.

Colin Where's the tea place?

Andy Down the corridor.

Colin Do you want some?

Joe Not from you. I don't know you.

Colin goes.

Hey. You, whatever your name is, you could have that
bike. Nobody would know. Clear off with it. I wouldn't
tell. And anyway I'm daft.
  This one wouldn't say, would you?
  Has anybody warned you about women?

Andy We've had talks about men.

Joe It's women you've got to watch. One stopped me the
other day. Cracked on she was selling flags. Flags! She
must have been sixty if she was a day. I said you ought to
be ashamed of yourself.

*Gilchrist takes no notice of this monologue as she
washes him.*

Ow.

Gilchrist Sorry.

Andy He's rude.

Gilchrist He's old. He's on tablets. Take no notice.

Joe Mind you, this one likes me. Do you know why?
Because I don't do it in my trousers. Isn't that so?

Gilchrist Well, it's not because of your qualities of mind
or your occasionally malodorous feet.

Joe I'm very good in that respect.

Gilchrist The feet?

Joe No. The lav. That's why I've lasted so long.

Gilchrist takes no notice as Colin returns.

Colin Out of order.

Joe Oh hello, Colin. Haven't seen you for a bit. To what do we owe the pleasure? I've just had a feller in here claiming he was you. A nancy. I said if he were my son I'd leather him. What must his mother feel?

Colin Maybe she doesn't care. Maybe she's dead.

Joe Have you bought me aught? Nothing? Not even a grape?

Colin I couldn't think of anything you'd want.

Joe A clean vest. When I was in once before, that's what your mam always brought. She was a good 'un.
  What're you got up like that for?

Colin I came on my bike.

Joe Oh, this lad's got a bike. Where from?

Colin London.

Joe If you're a civil servant, why aren't you in a suit? I tell people you're chauffeur-driven.

Colin It's the Minister that's chauffeur-driven. And I'm not a civil servant.

Gilchrist (*having finished*) Right. Done. Does that feel better?

Joe A bit.

Gilchrist So what do we say?

Joe We don't say anything. It's your job.

Colin Dad.

Joe mutters something.

Gilchrist I didn't hear it. You don't say it, you don't get something else.

She has taken out her iPhone.

Joe I am obliged to you, Sister Gilchrist, for washing me. We had showers in the pit. Not that you'd know that.

Gilchrist Good. Now . . .

Joe Not yet. I want the lav. Take me to the lav, please.

Gilchrist Do you want to take him?

Colin *No.* I don't.

Andy And I'm not.

Joe I can wipe my own bottom.

Gilchrist Yes, well we must be thankful for small mercies.

She wheels him out, leaving Andy and Colin.

Colin So who are you, pushing my dad around? A trainee?

Andy No fear. Work experience. What do you do?

Colin I'm a management consultant.

Andy Like a civil servant?

Colin Better.

Andy Got up like that?

Colin I cycle. I've won races. You like it here?

Andy The hospital?

Colin The town.

Andy It's where I live. I've never been anywhere else. What's London like?

Colin Beats this.

Andy Clubs and that?

Colin Clubs. Food. Everything.

Colin gives him a card.

If you find yourself down there, give me a call.

Andy You don't know me.

Colin No. Let's say you strike a chord.

Gilchrist wheels Joe back in as Andy rides out on the bike.

I was born here. I know what it's like.

Joe Now for the floor show.
That's why we get on. I sing out.

Gilchrist You're a model.

Joe The doctor says I've got the prostate of a twenty-year-old.

Gilchrist Right.

Gilchrist plugs her iPhone into some speakers. It plays dance music as she levers Joe out of his chair.

MUSIC: 'Love and Marriage'.

He dances with her in a beautiful olde-tyme dancing way. As they dance –

Colin He can't walk but he can dance still.

Gilchrist It happens.

Joe You're champion at this. Though it's old-fashioned.

Gilchrist That's why I like it.

Joe You were never tempted by disco?

Gilchrist With a chair at home? How?

Joe Pick of the partners here. Nobody dances like me. His mother never liked dancing.

Colin She didn't like you dancing. She liked you singing.

Joe He can sing, our Colin. Voice like an angel. Go on, sing.

He collapses as the camera crew plus Salter appear.

Salter Sister Gilchrist.

Gilchrist Too late. You've just missed Lionel Blair.

Salter This is what we're looking for.

Alex gives a thumbs up.

(*To camera.*) This woman (*i.e. Gilchrist*) does more for this hospital than its most dedicated surgeon. 'One of the old school,' people say. Do you know what I say? I say, 'Thank God for it.' We are fortunate in this hospital still to have our geriatric ward. Other keynote hospitals have long since hived them off. We cherish ours, as we cherish our Sister Gilchrist. (*To Gilchrist.*) Have you got a philosophy when it comes to old people?

Gilchrist No different from babies. The first priority is to keep them clean. And I don't mean clean as masked by air freshener . . . Pine Fragrance, Forest Glade . . . because you know that underneath there is the smell of urine – can I say that? – whereas I like my wards to smell of fresh air or smell of nothing at all.
Will that do?

Salter (*to camera*) Outspoken, perhaps, but a treasure. (*To Andy.*) Oi. You.

They move the bed.

(*Ushering out the camera crew.*) Trust Sister Gilchrist.
Beds in apple pie order
Apple pie in apple pie order. No dribbles.

Joan Collins, Shirley Bassey, neat, sweet-smelling and above all clean.

Colin and Joe are left.
Awkward silence.

Joe Your Auntie Violet came last week.

Colin Yeah?

Joe Just put her head round the door.

Colin You should have taken her picture.

Joe What for?

Colin She died three years ago.

Joe You don't like this place, do you? They told me. London wants to close it down.

Colin Maybe.

Joe I tell you, it's a sight better than the care home – The Cedars. They were all barmy. Here it's only some of them. And it was only with my chest being bad that I got in here.

Colin They say you'll be a lot better, once this infection's cleared up.

Joe I don't want to be better. Better means back to the care home. I don't know why I had to be put anywhere.

Colin Dad. You've forgotten. After Mam died, you couldn't look after yourself. Else you wouldn't. You didn't wash. You didn't eat. You used to wander the streets.

Joe I used to wander the streets? You were the one who used to wander the fucking streets. It didn't get you put in a home. It ought to have got you arrested. It's what killed your mam.

Colin It never was. It was coping with you.

Valentine approaches.

Joe Go away, you. You wouldn't understand this. This is father and son. Private.

Valentine Sorry. Sorry.

Joe Stuck in here with a load of old lasses. It's just lucky I'm easy to get on with.
Do you still do that?

Colin What?

Joe Go out on patrol. Walk the streets.

Colin No.

Joe Found what you were looking for?

Pause.

I'd something to tell you.

Pause.

Gone.
When I was in here years ago with appendicitis, I was on Mountbatten Ward. This time they put me on Dusty Springfield. So don't tell me there's been no progress. Oh, that's it.
That woman. The nurse. Gilchrist.

Colin She likes you . . . God knows why.

Joe I'll tell you why. It's because, when I want to go, I sing out. With her, it's a religion. (*He becomes furtive.*) I'll tell you something else an' all.

Colin Dad, if it's stuff about women, I don't want to know.

Andy has come in, still on the bike.

Joe Listen, I was a tally man down the pit. I know about keeping tabs and I've watched her . . . You've got to keep on the right side of her and I'll tell you for why –

Colin Dad. I won't listen. You're poorly.
Can you take him back?

Joe No. I haven't finished.

Colin (*calling after them*) I'll come in later on.

Andy pushes Joe off past Valentine, who, seeing the coast is clear, now approaches.

Valentine Alright, Joe?

Joe Bugger off.

Valentine We haven't met.

Colin No. Colin Colman. (*Peering at his name tag.*) Doctor . . .

Valentine Valentine.

Colin Unusual name.

Valentine My actual name is Valiyaveetil. I changed it because nobody could pronounce it.

Colin When was that?

Valentine When they let me in.

Colin Lucky.

Valentine Why?

Colin Much harder these days. Still, you're doing a good job.

Valentine I hope so.

Colin Though I wouldn't have thought that geriatrics was overcrowded.

Valentine I like old people. Your father's very proud of you. My son the civil servant.

Colin News to me.

Valentine That's fathers.

Colin And I'm not a civil servant. I just work in Whitehall.

Valentine Any news re the closure?

Colin If there is, nobody has told me.

Suddenly, there is uproar. Shouting. Valentine pushes Colin out of the way as a doctor, Fletcher, rushes through with a terrified patient in a wheelchair.

Fletcher Back. Back. Out of the fucking way.
Bed on Shirley Bassey! Bed on Shirley Bassey!

He rushes the wheelchair across the stage and they disappear. Valentine is unperturbed.

Valentine One of the innovations that commended itself to your Minister and which we hope went in our favour at the Inquiry was that, here at the Beth, the placement of patients, finding a patient a bed, has, in routine cases, been made the responsibility of the individual doctors. Emergencies, of course, are rather different.

Colin That looked like an emergency.

Valentine No, no. And the doctors like it, the young ones particularly.
It was a brainwave of Mr Salter's and I gather they're thinking of wheeling it out for the whole of the NHS. Beds after all are our main problem.

Colin Tell me about it. And where would that bed be coming from?

Valentine Geriatrics. Shirley Bassey, Dusty Springfield. There's been a death . . . And death means a bed.

Colin Which a larger establishment would probably have anyway.

Valentine Maybe, But patients love this hospital. It doesn't scare them as some hospitals do.

Colin It scares me. We don't like small.

Valentine We?

Colin People like me, who are trying to wrench the NHS on to a sensible footing. We don't like cosy.

Valentine Patients do. The cosy, the familiar. Same doctors, same faces. And on our wards in particular, if the doctor is familiar, and perhaps even more the nurse, then death may be less unfamiliar too.

Colin Cosy is lazy. Cosy means stagnation.

Valentine Not altogether. Are you familiar with the notion of peristalsis?

Colin I am not a doctor. I know nothing of medicine. Peri-what?

Valentine Peristalsis is the involuntary contraction and relaxation of the intestines, whereby the contents of the gut move through the body –

He clenches and unclenches his hand in demonstration.

A hospital has its own peristalsis in the way that patients are admitted, are treated, recover and move on, or die and don't. Either way it's movement. Not stagnation.

Colin Except if the hospital is like a body and the patients move through, it's the geriatric wards in particular where patients are more likely to take their leave. Geriatrics is the arsehole of the hospital and patients are the shit.

Valentine So Whitehall seems to think.

Colin I am not Whitehall. I am an independent consultant.

Fletcher comes through, with his patient still in the wheelchair, followed by Ramesh who has got the bed and is indeed pushing his patient in it.

Fletcher Fuck, fuck, fuck.

Ramesh (*the winner*) Finger on the pulse, finger on the pulse.

They go off.
  Salter comes in, a little flustered.

Salter Mr Colman, Mr Colman. Mervyn Salter, Chairman of the Trust. Sister Gilchrist put me in the picture. Can you forgive me? Welcome, welcome.
  Valentine, do you know who this is?

Valentine Mr Colman's son?

Salter Yes, yes. Our own Mr Colman. But on the larger stage. A messenger from on high.

Salter Do you bring news?

Colin This is a private visit.

Salter Of course, of course. I understand, only I was hoping you were going to make us all very happy.

Colin perhaps re-parks his bike.

(*To Valentine.*) Why wasn't I told? But what is he wearing? I thought he was the window cleaner.

Colin I'm here to see my father. He hasn't been well.

Salter Well, of course. Otherwise he wouldn't be here.

Valentine Like many ex-miners Mr Colman is suffering from pneumoconiosis and currently has a bladder infection.

Salter Oh dear.

34

Valentine But with the right treatment we're hopeful he'll improve.

Valentine leaves.

Salter Quite so.

Valentine Good to meet you.

Salter Be reassured, Mr Colman. Incidentally, we have splendid new parking facilities for bikes, did Valentine not tell you? CCTV supervision, everything. We don't want your precious metalwork to come to any harm. Did you come a long way?

Colin (*as if it's obvious*) From London.

Salter From London! I hope you've been offered some tea. Sponsored, were you?

Colin No, just exercise.

Salter Because there's nothing you can tell me about sponsoring, not after our campaign. A new world to me. A revelation. No, a liberation. I surprised myself. Drag, woad, panto. All for the hospital, and these wards in particular.

Can you see me as Queen Victoria?

No, I couldn't. But that was only the beginning. Only everybody was doing it. Knitting, swimming, jogging. Sky-diving, moi! The community owes you a great deal.

Colin Not me.

Salter And me personally. Would you believe it, I used to be shy?

Whatever the outcome, this campaign has brought the whole town together. We need our geriatric wards. We need our hospital. Now it all depends on the Minister.

Did he seem pleased? Because he loved the choir. And the way we've renamed the wards.

Colin Oh yes. *He* was over the moon.

Salter But you weren't?

Colin Mr Salter. The notion of a hospital catering for a community from birth to death is a sentimental one. It's the stuff of television. We do not need these birth-to-death emporiums. And I speak as one who was born here and whose father will, if it survives, die here.

Salter I don't remember you from the Inquiry.

Colin Fortunately for you, I was otherwise engaged, closing down a hospital in Hampshire.

Salter So where, in your view, are we going wrong?
  We are well run. Efficient. We even make a profit. What else is there?

Colin Centres of excellence. Specialist units. What does this 'plucky little hospital' specialise in?

Salter It's not as if we haven't tried. We put in for a cancer centre but unfortunately Leeds had bagged that, and nothing else has quite the same glamour. Huddersfield had nabbed the kidney and Doncaster, of all places, the liver. Our only available option was dermatology, which nobody was keen on. So perforce, we had to concentrate on being lifelong – which we'd always been – and an all-purpose local hospital. Nursing. Patient care. What people want. And our figures are good. Ward for ward, we are up there with the flagship hospitals.

Colin Oh, I agree. Your figures are excellent.

Salter Did you not see all the awards in the foyer?
  You shake your head?

Colin Small, badly run and in the red, it would undoubtedly close. Efficiently run and meeting its targets, it should close too, because, if it is profitable, why is it not in the private sector? We cannot afford hospitals like this.

Salter Not if we put the shutters up in Joan Collins and Dusty Springfield we can't.

Of course, it's always touch and go. No beating about the bush – old people are unpredictable. They can't always be relied on to throw in the towel to order. But we need them. Without these wards, we might not always meet out targets.

Colin Exactly. So they should go.

Salter You don't want us to meet our targets?

Colin Mr Salter, let me be plain. The State should not be seen to work. If the State is seen to work, we shall never be rid of it.

Salter I take it the Minister does not share your views?

Colin On the contrary, he originated them. Why do you think he's in the job?

Salter To reprieve the Beth would do him no harm. This is his constituency after all. His majority is, to say the least, precarious. Close it and I wouldn't vote for him.

Colin I am not privy to his thoughts but faced with the resistance of the entire community, sky-diving and such like antics, of course he may capitulate.

I have worked very hard to close this place down. I thought it was in the bag. If he caves in now, it will be heart-breaking.

Salter I sympathise.

An eruption of old people singing and dancing.

MUSIC: 'Good Morning' (from *Singin' in the Rain*).

The camera crew comes through and, trailing behind the singers, Mary, who is holding a drip stand. Mary sits in a chair, attended by Valentine.

Mary If you don't know the words, they tell you to la-la. I could la-la everything. My whole life could have been la-la.

Salter takes a seat by Mary.

I could tell you something about that seat only I won't.

Salter gets up again smartish.

Colin Why the filming?

Salter It's part of our campaign. A documentary to commemorate . . . to flag up, if you like, the survival of the hospital. We figured that the more publicity we had, the harder we would be to close.

Colin Quite.

Salter It'll be shown on Pennine People. Be assured it's only local.

Colin There is no such thing as local. The world is local.

Valentine They're also here to film the ceremony.

Colin What ceremony?

Valentine The presentation of the Bywater Medal to Sister Gilchrist.

Salter Twenty-five years' unblemished service.

Valentine Perhaps Mr Colman would do it?

Salter Oh. I was hoping that was going to be me.

Valentine Perhaps Mr Colman could even sing. The choir will be singing. Your father tells me you have a lovely voice.

Colin My father seems to have told you a good deal.

Valentine No. Only that you liked singing.

38

Colin I did. When I was a boy, he conned me into joining the colliery choir, doing fundraising.

Salter Were you a miner?

Colin No. I failed the oral. You should have asked the Minister.

Salter Why, does he sing?

Colin No, but he's a politician. He loves all that . . . presenting prizes, opening stuff . . . he'd cross London just to open a jam jar.

Salter Well you are speaking to an ex-mayor (twice over, did I say). I understand that. One is just happy to be of service.

Colin cycles off, followed by Salter. Valentine is still with Mary, checks her blood pressure, holds her hand.

Valentine Mary, you could be a teenager.

Mary I thought when I was old I'd stop bothering what other folks thought. It's been the bane of my life has that. Doing what was expected of me. I was a librarian. I looked after my father. I thought when I was old I'd get my own way. Instead of which I got shingles.

Valentine Do you want a book? The trolley's about. I'm sure I can find you something.

Mary No. I can have my own way there at least. No more books.

Colin is on his mobile, in a corridor.

Colin George. It's me.
  Would you believe it, the fucking television's here.
  God knows. Some local outfit.
  No. Only don't let on to himself or he'll want to know why he wasn't invited.

39

Saw a nice-looking lad this morning, pushing my dad around. Longing to get away, you could tell. Me, fifteen years ago.

Incidentally, do you know what peristalsis means?

You do? I didn't.

Dad? Oh, he's alright.

Oh yes, that's the other thing. I had to help wash him, watch while the nurse bathed his bits.

Listen, twat face, you forget that I'm a working-class boy. Until today, I had never seen my dad's dick. Is that a rite of passage, seeing your dad's dick?

No.

Oh, average.

Yeah. Nothing to write home about. Not that I can imagine any circumstances in which my dad's dick would be something one would write home about.

Actually, I might come back. Now he's not going to peg out, I might as well.

No, I'll shove the bike on the train.

I'd forgotten how much I hate this place.

Elsewhere Fletcher corners Gilchrist.

Fletcher What happened to the phone call? I thought we had an understanding.

Gilchrist It's not always predictable.

Fletcher There's not anything I'm neglecting?

Gilchrist Such as what?

Fletcher Chocolates. The occasional bottle. Flowers. I gather Ramesh bunches you from time to time.

Gilchrist Doesn't do him any good. They go straight in the bin.

Fletcher So what do I do?

He puts his hand on her arm or her bum.

Gilchrist Not that. Just do your job.

Fletcher I'm trying to. A bit of advance warning wouldn't come amiss.

Gilchrist I don't know when they're going to go. I'm not God.

Fletcher God doesn't have targets. I'm three from the bottom.

Gilchrist Not my problem.

Fletcher Have you no weak spots?

Gilchrist (*removing his hand again*) If I do, that's not one of them.

All the old people are sitting round, Valentine busying himself with patients, and stroking their hands to reassure them. Gilchrist and Pinkney at work. Cliff and Alex filming.

Are you feeling more up to this now, Cora?

Cora I've got tummy ache still. I never thought I'd end up in a home.

Gilchrist You're not in a home. You're in hospital.

Mavis If she's not well enough, I can have another go. I've got lots to say.

Lucille And I have a wild side, which nobody has ever tapped.

Mavis Well you're leaving it a bit late.

Cora I've never done anything with my life. I've just been a housewife.

Pinkney Well that's not nothing. And isn't your son in Australia?

Cora He is.

Pinkney Well that's an achievement in itself.

Cora What I wanted to be was some sort of representative. Abroad preferably.

Pinkney What could you represent? What could she represent?

Mavis Cosmetics.

Lucille Cosmetics: why not reinforced concrete?

Mavis Don't be so daft. Concrete.

Lucille That's why, Mavis, you are behind the times. Us women can do anything now.

Joe Yes, and they can keep their mouths shut. I had ten men under me.

Lucille So did I on a good day.

Joe I want the lav again.

One of the nurses wheels him away.

I wish I could stop going. I've got an arse like a sauce bottle top.

Cliff Cut.

Neville Cora, which is your bad ear?

Cora (*tapping her knee*) This one.

Neville What sort of pain is it in your tummy? Is it just in the one place? Because I've had that.

And what was it?

Neville Nerves. It's always been nerves with me.

Cora They never tell you, do they? You'd think at this age you'd stop caring, only you don't.

Neville No.

Valentine and Gilchrist leave, Valentine blowing them a kiss.

Lucille He's a bit touchy-feely, that Dr Valentine.

Mavis Is he? I'm used to that, I tend to bring it out in people. Mind you, I don't mind it. God knows nobody else is doing it.

Lucille He's no business holding your hand or stroking your arm. What's that about? After all, we're still women.

Mavis Only just. Dirty Gertie never lays a finger on you except to see if you've wet your knickers.

Mary Well . . .

Mavis What, Mary? Spit it out.

Mary It's not as if he's a vicar. They're supposed to touch you, doctors.

Lucille Only up to a point.

Cora He rubs my back sometimes, but it's only to fetch the wind up.

Lucille Well, fondling folks, I think he wants reporting.

Gilchrist Rosemary. Mrs Maudsley, admitted this morning . . .

Pinkney Yes? What did I do?

Gilchrist It's not what you did. It's what you didn't do. That's what you did. You're supposed to check.

Pinkney I was going to. Her daughter said there was no problem.

Gilchrist She would. She was sodden.

Pinkney She still has a lovely voice.

Gilchrist Rosemary. We aren't running a choral society. I am trying to run a dry ward. The singing is incidental.

Pinkney I'm sorry, Sister Gilchrist, but I want them to think that life still has something to offer . . . Singing, games, give them something to look forward to. Give them something else to look forward to.

Gilchrist Sat in wet clothes, what you look forward to is being dry.
    Baking them birthday cakes, kissing and cuddling them . . . Maybe I was like that when I first started.

Pinkney Well, you have your favourites.

Gilchrist No. I have my unfavourites.

Pinkney And we all know who they are. On your list.

Gilchrist My lisr is just a nursing aid. If anybody has a little accident, I want telling.

Pinkney I thought you didn't believe in little accidents.

Gilchrist I don't. I believe in accident prevention. Catch them in time and you save on laundry bills.

Maybe some of the old people start to sing softly.

Pinkney I love them all. Maybe we complement each other. The hard and the soft. Like policemen.

Gilchrist I don't know that giving them stuff to look forward to is doing them any favours.
    Singing and what-not . . . It encourages them to think that life might still have something to offer beyond the next dollop of turkey mince. That there is a world beyond Angel Delight.

Pinkney I just wish we could have pets. Give them something to stroke, be responsible for. A cat maybe, but babies would be best. Old people love babies, and when they can't talk, they can still talk to babies.

Gilchrist Do you know what babies mean to me now? More shit.

Pinkney rehearses a song with a group of the old people.

MUSIC: 'Sunny Side of the Street' (Louis Armstrong).

Colin, now changed out of Lycra, but still with his bike, comes in to say goodbye to Joe.

Colin I'm glad to see you looking better.

Joe I don't want to look better. Look better, they boot you out.

Colin (*looking at his phone*) I'm wanted in London. The Minister wants his hand holding.

Joe He's not one as well?

Colin Dad, it's a figure of speech.
Threat of a strike.

Joe Who by?

Colin Doctors.

Joe You see, I could help you there. I was a tally man. They want to ask me. I did all that.
Pickets. Colliery gates.

Colin Dad, you forget. I'm on the other side.

Joe Horses? Truncheons out?

Colin No such luck. Just sitting round a table.

Joe Holding hands.
He can sing, you know.

Colin I never can. Not now.

Joe You can. He sang in the colliery choir.

Colin You made me.

45

Joe He sang at concerts. He helped raise money.

Colin Only because you pretended it was a good cause.

Pinkney Well this is a good cause. Go on. Be a sport.

Joe Go on, kid. Do it for me. Do it for your mam.

Colin sings.

MUSIC: 'Blow the Wind Southerly'.

Joe then has a bad attack of coughing which Dr Valentine attends to. Then Gilchrist pulls Colin aside.

Gilchrist I'd like to run it like a real hospital.

Colin How do you mean?

Gilchrist To my mind having a choir is an admission of failure. Patients shouldn't stick around long enough to make up a choir. This isn't a home. It's a hospital. And in a real hospital, better, you'd be discharged. Here half of them have nowhere to be discharged to.

Colin The community?

Gilchrist Don't make me laugh. The council care homes are full and when the private ones aren't it's because they charge the earth.

Colin That's not really our baby.

Gilchrist Well, whose baby is it? It's got to be somebody's baby. I'd like to be a nurse, not a skivvy. Get folks well, old as they are, and send them out. Make the place work.

Colin I keep being told it does work.

Gilchrist Just.
You don't see the queues, the full wards, the beds blocked.
Nothing moves.

Colin It's a hospital. You can't just look at it in terms of through-put and turnover.

Gilchrist That's an admission coming from you. Are you having second thoughts? Two minds?

Colin Two minds went out with Mrs Thatcher.
   Seeing my dad. I know how I ended up where I am. When I was a kid I had to be on their side. But how could I be when every fucking day it was drummed into me about Mrs T closing down the pits? And it didn't help that he was right she was lying. But God it was so dreary. So of course you're young and you go the other way. That's what he can't forgive.

Ambrose (*speaking for the first time*) I wish you'd have been in my class. I could have put you straight, changed your mind.

Gilchrist Bit late now.

   Salter comes on.

Salter Mr Colman.

Colin I'm needed at the coalface.

Salter Off already? I'm glad I caught you.

Colin When it comes to the decision, you should remember that most politicians are cowards. Is that reassuring?

Salter It is.
   However, if you're talking to the Minister, make sure you tell him that we've followed his advice renaming the wards and how grateful we are . . .

Colin Yes?

Salter Plus I'd count it a courtesy were you to emphasise how keenly one sympathises with his predicament and should he decide that closure is unavoidable one hopes that my experience and goodwill might be found useful in some other capacity. If you understand me.

Colin I think I do.

Salter Travel safely.
Settling in, Mrs Maudsley?

Mrs Maudsley It was my house!

Salter Quite so.

Salter goes. Colin goes back to Joe.

Colin I'm off back to London, Dad.

Joe You've only just got here. There was something else. What was it?

Colin I'll miss my train.

He tries to kiss his father.

Joe Gerroff.

Colin Dad, everybody kisses now.

Joe Not up here.

Colin It doesn't mean anything.

Joe So why do it?
Off you go. Mind on your bike.

Alex and Cliff are filming. Gerald is attending to Mavis.

Alex Do you *like* singing?

Mavis I do, but then I'm more artistic. You do, don't you, Mrs Maudsley?

Mrs Maudsley I've got something to tell you.

Mavis We know it was your house, love, but besides that, you liked singing.

Mrs Maudsley Did I?

Mavis You were the Pudsey Nightingale.

Mrs Maudsley It wasn't just Pudsey. I went all over, singing at different dos. I sang in . . . somewhere beginning with S . . .

Joe Stockholm?

Mrs Maudsley Stockport.

Lucille To be honest I don't much – like singing. Only it keeps her happy.

Neville Who?

Lucille Bouncing Betty. She thinks it takes your mind off things. Busy busy busy.

Neville Singing takes it out of me a bit.

Joe Tell you what would take it out of you. Hacking away with a pick and shovel half the day.
     Singing, it's nowt.

Molly starts banging her tray.

Mavis Get lost, Molly.

Gerald It's alright, Mavis.

Mavis He likes me, does Gerald.

Lucille I'm the one he likes. I'm his favourite.

Alex (*to Cliff*) This is no good. It's all so fucking nice. What we need is dirt.
     Do you remember when we did that pig farm thing for Anglia, where we thought the pigs were being fed hospital waste – and we kitted the two lads out with camcorders.

Cliff I've still got one. The thieving little sods nicked the other.

49

Alex It won't be Steadicam with this lot . . . (*He mimes trembling with the camera.*) Still, worth a try.

Look, boys and girls.

Joe We're not boys and girls.

Alex Quite right. Ladies and gentleman.

Mavis Oooh.

Alex Has anyone ever handled a camera?

Mavis Snaps? Of course.

Lucille I have. Our Joseph filmed me for a school project.

Alex But you've never done it?

Lucille I'm eighty-four.

Mary I have.

Lucille You? How?

Mary At the library. I often did it. Manuscripts and one thing and another. Camera just like that. I'm not just a pretty face.

Cliff Right, darling. You're on the team.

Ambrose Very Free Cinema.

Cliff Just keep your eyes open for anything that's funny.

Mary Funny ha-ha?

Alex More funny peculiar.

Mary Sex, you mean?

Alex No. Well, yes, if there is any.

Mary I don't want to get anyone into bother.

Cliff You won't, love. It's just for the film.

Alex All in aid of the hospital. (*To Valentine.*) Now, OK with you, Doctor, if we get them talking about their memories?

Valentine What sort of memories?

Alex Work, for a start.

Valentine Sure.

Alex Did you all go out to work?

Hazel I did.

Cora I didn't.

Mary You had to do.

Hazel I worked in Stylo shoe shop for a bit. Then Gallons and the Maypole. And I did a bit at Timothy White's before it changed hands.

Alex Then what?

Hazel I got married.

Lucille I live the high life. Many's the knicker I've had to retrieve from the chandelier in that house.

Mavis Where?

Lucille Leeds.

Mavis We're talking about work.

Lucille It was work. Men. Men. Men.

Valentine (*embarrassed*) Who's got grandchildren?

Cora One of mine's a fully qualified market gardener.

Mavis Our Kirsty's a dental hygienist. She'd do my teeth only I don't have any.

Lucille I've got grandchildren only they never come near. One's called Emily, which used to be a right ordinary name only now it's more of an upmarket name. Joseph's the same. Our Eileen's got a Joseph. He's a right demon. That's the school's fault, I think. When I went to elementary school, they sat us down and made us learn.

51

Alex Learn what?

Lucille Poetry for a start. I used to know reams of poetry.

Joe I remember 'Eskimo Nell'.

Lucille That wasn't taught at school.

Joe We used to sing it in the bar at the Institute.

Alex What's the Institute?

Joe It was the club where we played snooker and whatnot.
  Carpet warehouse now.

Neville
  I wandered lonely as a cloud,
  That floats on high o'er vales and hills,
  When all at once I saw a crowd,
  A host of golden daffodils.

Valentine Very good, Neville.

Neville Ullswater that was. We once went up there on a mystery tour. It wasn't much. Give me Roundhay Park any day.

Mary
  And thou most kind and gentle Death,
  Waiting to hush our latest breath,
  O praise Him! Alleluia!
  Thou leadest home the child of God,
  And Christ our Lord the way hath trod.
  O praise Him! O praise Him!

  They all join in.

  Alleluia! Alleluia! Alleluia!

Mavis That doesn't count. That's a hymn.

Valentine Anything counts. It isn't a competition.

Joe Everything's a competition these days. Just ask my lad. Competition brings out the best in people. That's what Mrs Thatcher taught us apparently.

Valentine I've got a poem I like if I can find it.

He looks through his notebook, which should have been seen earlier.

It's called 'Ten Types of Hospital Visitor'.

Lucille Ten? We're lucky if we get one.

Valentine It's by a poet called . . .

Ambrose Charles Causley. He once gave a talk at our school. Is he still with us?

Valentine I don't think so.
  He talks about all the visitors you don't want to see, but this is the ideal visitor.

The sixth visitor says little,
Breathes reassurance,
Smiles securely.
Carries no black passport of grapes
And visa of chocolate. Has a clutch
Of clean washing.
Unobtrusively stows it
In the locker; searches out more.
Talks quietly to the Sister
Out of sight, out of earshot, of the patient.
Arrives punctually as a tide.
Does not stay the whole hour.

Even when she has gone
The patient seems to sense her there:
An upholding
Presence.

Ambrose What about the last verse?

Valentine I'm not sure we want it. Why? Do you know it?

Ambrose Yes, it's very short.

The tenth visitor
Is not usually named.

Pinkney Well I think that's morbid. We're better off singing.

They sing.

MUSIC: 'Blow the Wind Southerly' (reprise).

Fletcher Do you know what I dream of?

Ramesh I never sleep.

Fletcher A bed.

Ramesh Who with?

Fletcher With nobody. An empty fucking bed. A vacancy. I haven't had a bonus in weeks. What's the secret?

Ramesh Charm?

Fletcher Bollocks. Who do you have to fuck? Because I know it's not Gilchrist.

Ramesh A smile knows no frontiers.

Fletcher I'm getting desperate. Currently, I have one patient in an ambulance in the long-stay car park, two in the corridor by the bins, and when we were really desperate last week I stashed somebody in the mortuary.

Ramesh Dead?

Fletcher No. It's called thinking outside the box.

Ramesh It's no good. We can't go on like this. We're going to have to widen our horizons.

54

Fletcher How?

Ramesh (*and he's said this many times before*) The private sector.

Fletcher Where? Where?

Stage dark, apart from the lights on the nurses' station. Gilchrist at the desk. Valentine, having done the ward round, is signing it off.

Gilchrist This is the time I like. When you've done the handover, been round with the trolley and they're all tucked up, clean and dry. Sometimes on a night, if you open the window, you can smell the moors.

Valentine None of that at Tadcaster. I'm told the windows don't even open.
  Will you miss it?

Gilchrist Nursing? No. That's what people pretend is a vocation and it's just the place where they've ended up. No choice to it.
  Dr Valentine. Can I show you something?

She fishes out a piece of paper.

Valentine Sure.

Gilchrist It's only rough and the spelling's all over the place only it's what I thought I could say when they give me the medal.

Valentine Spelling doesn't matter . . . what's this?

He shows it to her.

Gilchrist It's meant to be 'apprenticeship'. It doesn't seem stupid?

Valentine No, course it doesn't.

Gilchrist And I don't sound like a freak?

Valentine Sister Gilchrist . . .

Gilchrist You never call me Alma.

Valentine Nobody does. Can I?

Gilchrist You can if you want. Though not in front of the others.

Valentine Alma, you say you were no good at exams. You should have got help.

Gilchrist I'd have had to ask. I didn't want to be beholden. And I didn't want to let on. I don't want to be in anybody's pocket.

Valentine I can understand that.

Gilchrist You must have been good at exams.

Valentine The medical ones were alright.

Gilchrist Why, what other ones are there?

Pause.

Valentine I thought they'd forgotten me, only now some question has arisen over my status.

Gilchrist Are you not a proper doctor?

Valentine Oh no. Not that status.
It's what they're supposed to do, employers . . . check up on . . . whether one has a right to be here.

Gilchrist Even if you're a doctor?

Valentine Even if you're Archbishop of York. My hearing's over at Pontefract. I haven't told anyone, though Ambrose has been helping me a bit without understanding why. We shall see.

He pats her hand.

Gilchrist I hope when they give me this medal they won't ask me what lessons I've learned.

Valentine And if they do?

Gilchrist I would say that, if there was one lesson I've learned, it's don't leave it too late to die.
  These did.

Valentine A doctor can't say that.

Gilchrist (*she takes his hand*) Nurses can. Nurses do.

Valentine Have a quiet night.

  He goes. Gilchrist remains seated at the desk and there is silence, broken by . . .

Mrs Maudsley (*calling out*) It was my house. It was my house.

  Gilchrist stands up to see whose bed it is. She sits for a moment, before getting on the mobile.

Gilchrist Ramesh. It's me.
  Just to put you on standby. We may lose somebody on Shirley Bassey. Try me later on.

Mrs Maudsley (*calling out*) It was my house.

  Gilchrist takes something from her drawer. She hesitates with some sort of weighing-up going on.
    Then, priming it as she goes, she holds it up to the light so that we see it is a syringe.
    But what we also see is Mary holding her camcorder sneaking a shot of what is happening.
    End of Part One.

Part Two

MUSIC: 'Good Golly, Miss Molly' (Little Richard).

The old people – in a memory of their younger selves – perform a full-out song and dance. Then:
  Mr and Mrs Earnshaw with Salter and Valentine.

Earnshaw Stay alive . . . That's all she had to do. Three months.

Mrs Earnshaw We should have kept her at home. I said.

Earnshaw It's a hospital. Keeping you alive is what they do. She's done it on purpose. She never liked me.

  The camera crew is trying to sneak in but is blocked by Salter.

Salter Sorry, sorry. Private grief. Private grief.

Earnshaw Come on in. Come on in. I don't mind.

Salter No, no. These are heartbroken people. We have a duty of care. Dr Valentine.

Earnshaw Why? Weeping? There's nothing you lot like better.

  But Valentine ushers the crew out, before coming back himself.

I want to know why.

Salter Death is a mystery.
  It's the question loved ones so often ask: why?

Earnshaw Not – (*Eyes up to heaven.*) Why? Why? (*Jabbing his finger.*)

58

Why, as soon as you got your hands on her, did this old lass in relatively good nick suddenly peg out?

Salter Well, she had gallstones and of course she was incontinent . . .

Earnshaw Listen, Doctor. I don't know much about medicine, but even I know you don't die of wet knickers.

Valentine She *was* eighty-eight.

Earnshaw That's no age nowadays. I read in the *Mail* that eighty is the new sixty. I want a post-mortem.

Salter Dr Valentine signed the death certificate.

Valentine She slept away. Try to think of it as a blessing.

Earnshaw A blessing to her maybe. Not to us. We've lost money. Where's the blessing in that?

Mrs Earnshaw (*weeping*) This was the Pudsey Nightingale.

Earnshaw Don't talk to me about the Pudsey Nightingale. I've never heard a nightingale, but if they are anything like your mother, I don't wonder they've become extinct.

Salter Who was on that night?

Valentine Alma. (*Correcting himself.*) Sister Gilchrist. She's a very experienced nurse.

Salter No one more so. She's up for the Bywater Medal

Earnshaw I don't care if she's up for the V fucking C. I want an inquiry.

Mrs Earnshaw We loved her

Earnshaw Love nothing. We want compensation.

Enter Pinkney with a bag.

Pinkney We thought you might like the contents of Mother's locker. A bottle of Lucozade, half full. An opened packet of Quality Street . . .

Mrs Earnshaw And what's that?

Pinkney A tissue with some rhubarb crumble she'd saved from supper.

Mrs Earnshaw She used to do that a lot, squat food. Said you never knew where your next meal was coming from.

Earnshaw We can use the Quality Street. Though knowing her, there'll be no soft centres. She'd always wolf them down first go off.

Mrs Earnshaw I think we'd like to donate the Lucozade, wouldn't we?

Earnshaw It's cost us a fortune, this. It's cost us my retirement. Where were we going? Not Spain. Not Marbella. Colwyn Bay.
   This is what you get for being modest in your aspirations. Robbed, that's what we've been. By an eighty-eight-year-old woman. It must be a record.

Salter I will show you out. Very often, I have to say, at this age there is no obvious cause of death

Earnshaw And if they do have a post-mortem, they won't find anything because I'll tell you what she died of . . . Spite.

Pinkney comes after them.

Pinkney You forgot your Quality Street.

Earnshaw shoves them viciously in his pocket as they go. The expelled camera has crept back.

Cliff Anything?

Valentine (*to camera*) Ordinarily, it has to be said, rage at the death of a loved one of advanced age is happily rare, with relief more often the norm . . . The whole business these days coming under the name of closure . . . Closure to the guilt of not having visited or only staying

60

half an hour when one does; closure to the boredom of talking to someone who is often incapable of talking back; closure to the boredom of having to talk to someone who is often disinclined to talk back. 'A blessing' is what relatives say. 'A happy release' . . . for everybody.

Thumbs up from Cliff. The camera withdraws. Gilchrist has come on.

Gilchrist And closure, too, to the unpermitted thoughts.

Valentine What are those?

Gilchrist The uncaring thoughts. The real thoughts of a carer.

Salter returns.

Salter You do have the death certificate?

Valentine Of course.

Salter And cause of death?

Valentine Whatever fancy name we choose to give it – old age.

Salter Quite so.
If he does make a complaint, he hasn't got a hope. Particularly so as ultimately any complaint ends up with me. The buck stops here. One feels almost sorry for them. Though at this age, most relatives are grateful.

Valentine (*drily*) They did donate the Lucozade.

Salter And post-mortems by request don't come cheap. These days they have to contribute.
Valentine, a word.
An entirely unrelated matter. I'm not in the slightest bit worried about this, but one of the ladies has seen fit not actually to complain but to suggest that you've been touching her . . . inappropriately, stroking her . . .

Valentine Stroking her what?

Salter No no. Not stroking her anything. Just . . . stroking her. Taking her hand. That sort of thing. Being affectionate.

Valentine And should I not?

Salter Oh no no. Of course you should. And some of the old biddies I'm sure appreciate it. After all they're not untouchables (sorry!) but what once upon a time would be called bedside manner these days borders on . . . interference.

Valentine I've been too loving?

Salter No–o. Though on another occasion you were seen to make an inappropriate gesture.

Valentine What sort of gesture?

Salter You . . . blew the old ladies a kiss.

Valentine That's forbidden?

Salter Just endeavour to be more detached. A whisker less affectionate. More . . . unfeeling. In a word, more professional.

Valentine Touching the patient has always seemed to me part of the treatment.

Salter Oh it is. It is. It's just a question of being less . . . well, remembering that you're a doctor, you can be less human.

Incidentally, we're in duty bound to enter this on your record, not that anything will happen. Just so that we're all of us in the clear.

Valentine Of course.

Back on the geriatric ward.

Hazel (*coming across Ambrose in his chair*) I like you, Gilbert. You're more refined. Do you want to go for a little ta-ta?

Ambrose My name's not Gilbert and no, I don't.

He reaches for his earphones, but she puts them out of reach.

Hazel No. We're practising the art of conversation. They've put me in this cardigan. I said to them: tangerine's a common colour.
  You've got lovely fingernails. Were you a dentist?

Ambrose gets hold of his earphones and puts them on.

I thought she was going to be someone a bit more classy, that Pudsey Nightingale. 'It was my house.' I said, give over. I was awake when she went. Next thing you know they're fetching on the trolley. Exit the Pudsey Nightingale.
  I've never heard a nightingale. Have you? You don't get them in industrial areas. I did hear a cuckoo once only that was over towards Harrogate where you could understand it.

Ambrose has taken off the earphones in despair. Valentine comes on, and Ambrose wildly signals for help.

Valentine Hazel. You're wanted.

Hazel Me? Me and Gilbert were just having a nice little chat.

Valentine Pop along to Shirley Bassey. Do you know where that is?

Hazel Course. Shirley Bassey was Princess Margaret. I'm not barmy.

She goes.

Ambrose One wonders how it is Hazel has managed to survive so long without being throttled.
  I'm not barmy, am I?

Valentine No.

Ambrose Am I a joke?

Valentine Ambrose, you're old, that's all. Are you still expecting your visitor?

Ambrose Well, he hasn't been.

Valentine That's good though, isn't it? The important thing is to have something to look forward to.

Ambrose Yes. I wish I could just slip away like Mrs Maudsley. Only life has one in its jaws and it doesn't give one up without a struggle. They talk about the jaws of death. Well, it's not death that has jaws. It's life. And now, here comes pain with its gull's beak.

Valentine We'll get you a tablet.

He wheels Ambrose away.

Mavis Has he ever mentioned a Mrs Ambrose?

Lucille Not to my knowledge.

Mavis That's sad.

Lucille Maybe he's not cut out for it.

Mavis What?

Lucille Marriage.

Mavis Course, when we first started, marriage was still the gateway to sexual intercourse.

Lucille Well, yes and no. I jumped the gun a bit. What was yours like?

Mavis Ellis?
He'd been well brought up.
He always asked first and said thank you afterwards.
Which is all you want really.

Lucille What did you call it?

Mavis We didn't call it anything.
We didn't talk about it.

Lucille We never talked about anything else. Except football. I had three husbands, all of them football mad.
I'd outlaw football.

Mavis With Ellis it was pigeons. Pigeons and model aeroplanes.

Lucille Pigeons. Football. Still, it was better than this.

Andy wheels Joe into the ward.

Andy Here we are again. Fatima Whitbread.

Joe So. Have you worked out any more small talk?

Andy shrugs.

Actually, never mind small talk, I'm busting for my bottle. Where is it?

Andy I'm not sure if I should be giving it to you.

Joe Why not? Give us it here.

Andy Health and Safety.

Joe I'm busting.

Andy holds it out, then takes it back

Andy What do you say?

Joe No, you little sod. Give us it here.

Andy A little word? Beg. Beg.

Joe Please, you rotten bugger.

He gives him it and Joe pees.

Andy 'Thank you'?

Joe 'Thank you' my arse. You don't belong in a hospital, you. You ought to be in a Borstal.

Andy Borstal? I've got a GCSE.

Joe So what? Our Colin's got ten, not to mention the ones that come after.

Andy What?

Joe A-Levels. Four. Starred.
You must be sorry the mines have gone, you.

Andy Why?

Joe Because they let you in no questions asked. You, you're going nowhere. One won't get you far.

Andy They've done you in, though, haven't they?

Joe What?

Andy The mines.

Joe I was happy.

Andy And now you're an invalid.
I bet at your Colin's work they don't all pile into the baths like you did. He won't be scrubbing the Minister's back.

Joe He's scrubbing it already.

Andy He'd probably have been happier doing all that.

Joe All what?

Andy Showers and that.

Joe What's that supposed to mean?

Andy All that Lycra and stuff. That's what he likes. Is that why he went off to London?

Joe (*does some of this bring on his coughing?*) You dirty-minded little arsehole.

66

Andy 'Have a go on my bike.' We know what that means. He was trying it on.

Joe Our Colin? He never was. And if he was, it wouldn't be with you.

Andy Who would it be with? Another Mr Ten-A-Levels? He doesn't realise things have changed up here. There's gay clubs in Barnsley these days. That's where they scrub each other's backs now.

Joe Where is she?

Andy Who?

Joe That nurse. She was due to cut my toenails.

Andy You're an old fart, you. What're you doing in hospital? My grandad's not in hospital and he's older than you.

Joe I have a rare disease.

Andy Bollocks.

He jigs the wheelchair about.

Joe Stop jogging me.

Andy Why, do you not like it?

He does it more.

Joe I'm entitled to respect.

Andy You're old. You're entitled to fuck-all. Here.

He gets the pee bottle and starts taunting him with it.

Joe Leave off. It's splashing me.

Andy Oh dear. I am sorry. I've spilled a bit. Butterfingers.

He sloshes the contents of the bottle over Joe.

Joe Get off. Stop it, you rotten bugger.

Andy You're lucky it's your own, not mine.

Joe Help. Nurse!

Pinkney comes in.

Pinkney What is it? What're you shouting about Joe?

Joe I'm all wet.

Andy If he'd said, I'd have taken him.

Joe This, it's not me. Honestly. It's him.

Andy Can I help?

Pinkney No, I'll see to him.

Andy clears off.

Joe It was him, the blighter.

Pinkney I thought he was your friend.

Joe So did I. He poured it over me.

Pinkney Never.

Joe He was showing off. It was him. It wasn't me.

Pinkney You've only wet your 'jamas. It's not a tragedy.

Joe It is for me.

Pinkney Why?

Joe If it goes down on her list, I'm done for.

Pinkney Don't be so silly. Only I'll have to tell her.

Joe Why? You could just change me. Come on. Be sharp and she won't know.

Pinkney is already on her mobile.

Pinkney It's Rosemary. Have you got a minute? Fatima Whitbread.

Joe No. No.

Pinkney She keeps a record. She has to know.

Joe Her list.

Pinkney It's part of her economy drive.

Enter Gilchrist.

Gilchrist What is it?

Pinkney I'm afraid Joe's had a little accident.

Joe I never have.

Gilchrist Joe? This isn't like you.

Pinkney I thought I'd better tell you.

Gilchrist You did right. Dear me, Joe. I don't know.
You're all the same in the end.

Joe It's not me, this. Honestly. It's him, the little monkey.
He did it. The lying little sod. He poured it all over me.

Gilchrist And why would he do that?

Joe Out of devilment. It's the way they are when they're
young.

Pinkney Andrew? No. He's got a GCSE.

Gilchrist I'm disappointed in you, Joe. You've spoiled
your record.
   And my dancing partner. I don't want a partner who
wets himself.

Pinkney We'll get you some dry things. I'm sorry.

Joe Judas.

*Later. The ward. Night. Gilchrist, alone on stage,
makes a phone call.*

Gilchrist Ramesh. Don't get over-excited. We may have a bed coming up.

Tonight or first thing.

I'll be in touch.

MUSIC: a pre-echo of the waltz that Gilchrist and Joe will dance later.

Two of the old ladies dance.

Joe talks to his son on his mobile under the bedclothes.

Joe It's your dad.

Where do you think I am? I'm in bed. On the ward. Where are you?

A box? What kind of a box?

The opera? I didn't know you liked opera.

If you don't, why do you go?

You're with the Health Secretary? Does he like opera?

Well, why does he go then?

Who lends him the box? Pharmaceuticals? Do they like opera?

Speak up. What's all that going on?

Tosca?

No, I don't want to listen. You listen to me. I'm ringing to say goodbye.

I may not be here in the morning.

Why? Because I'm like a trophy. The longest-living patient. The King of the Jungle. I'm on her list. I thought she liked me.

Don't 'Dad' me.

Why have you got to go?

What big number?

She stabs him? What did he do? Wet himself?

What's it about?

Love.

I bet that's not cheap, a box.

Opera in the Minister's box. Goodbye, Colin. You've come a long way.

Gilchrist in the ward with a mug of milk.

Joe Here you are, Alma, prowling the ward.

Gilchrist I don't prowl. I patrol.
Good news.

Joe Yes?

Gilchrist Your infection's cleared up.

Joe Why is that good news?

Gilchrist You're much better. You're eligible for discharge.

Joe When?

Gilchrist Tomorrow.

Joe Tomorrow? No. Where do I go? There's no room at The Cedars.

Gilchrist That's what I thought. Only you're in luck. Someone's died.

Joe He's the lucky one. It's a bin. I'm not going back there. I'm not.

Gilchrist Drink your milk.

Joe I liked us dancing.

Gilchrist Same here.

Joe Do you want a go now?

Gilchrist If we're quiet.

They dance.

MUSIC: 'I Can Give You the Starlight' (Ivor Novello).

Joe (*as they finish*) It's the last waltz.

Gilchrist Don't be so daft.

Joe I'll miss you getting your medal.

Gilchrist No.

Joe With going to The Cedars.

Gilchrist Oh yes. Well, never mind.
Aren't you going to drink your milk?

He doesn't say anything.

Well, it's there if you want it.
Goodnight. God bless.

The scene ends with him staring at the milk.

*Colin, Valentine, Salter and Gilchrist, the following
day. Colin in suit and his office clothes, having plainly
just arrived.*

Colin I was sympathetic up to a point, but I was in the
middle of an important meeting. I wasn't free to talk.

Gilchrist Your father said you were at the opera. *Tosca.*

Colin Yes.

Gilchrist With the Health Secretary.

Colin We had things to discuss. The opera was incidental.
What else did he say?

Gilchrist He was very proud, but he was upset you
couldn't talk.

Colin I did talk.

Gilchrist I left him a cup of something. To settle him
down.

Colin What sort of something?

Gilchrist Milk. Hot milk.

Colin He said he was going to die. He was on a list.

Salter I have to say, Mr Colman, such fantasies are not unusual.

Valentine And he had been ill. A chest infection. Which would make him vulnerable to quicker deterioration.

Colin He was in fear of his life.

Salter Patients often feel threatened, imagine that their belongings have been taken, for instance, the world a hostile place.

Colin Have there been other unexplained deaths?

Salter Valentine?

Valentine To die at eighty-six is hardly unexplained.

Colin What are the figures? How does the death rate compare with that in equivalent institutions?

There is a silence.

Don't you know?

Salter Valentine?

Valentine I don't have the figures at my fingertips. Comparing like for like, I should be surprised if they were unusual.

Colin Any spike? Five minutes on the computer would tell you.

Valentine Supposing the figures were high, geriatrics is the end. People die.

Gilchrist And, the ward was immaculate. What relatives came to visit remarked on it.

Salter And no one ever complained.

Valentine No, though . . .

Colin Though what?

Salter What Valentine is referring to is a complaint, specious in my view, over a patient – Mrs Maudsley – her daughter and son-in-law having found themselves disadvantaged by Mrs Maudsley's decease and are seeking compensation from the hospital.

Colin Do you carry out post-mortems?

Valentine Not invariably.

Colin 'Not invariably'?

Valentine Not usually. These were patients in their eighties and nineties.

Colin So you keep saying. Who signed the death certificates?

Salter Dr Valentine, naturally.

Valentine It was a matter of course. Here, death is no stranger.

Salter Sister Gilchrist, have you anything to add?

Gilchrist I am not sure what is being suggested. That I was negligent?

Valentine Or that I was?

Colin I am not suggesting anything. Like any other grieving relative, I would just like some answers.

Colin on the mobile to George as the old people assemble.

It's what I thought about this place from the start. It's too cosy.

They're having an inquest on this other old lass, Mrs Maudsley, but only because the family kicked up. If I want one I shall have to wait on that.

Course I do. Bring it on.

74

I know my father's dead, George. But on the plus side, none of this is going to do the hospital any good.

MUSIC: 'Sunny Side of the Street'.

Mary approaches Cliff with the camcorder.

Cliff Hello, darling.

Mary She seemed right as rain. Still going on about her house. I don't want to get anybody into trouble.

Ambrose I do apologise but I'm afraid I can't be there at your presentation.

Gilchrist No problem. I wish I didn't have to be there myself.

Ambrose The truth is I'm expecting a visit from one of my old pupils. He's just got back from . . .

Gilchrist You don't want your bag emptying?

Ambrose Addis Ababa.

Pinkney (*starts to wheel him into position*) Where did you say?

Ambrose Addis Ababa.

Pinkney Oh, he won't be coming now.

Ambrose Why? We don't know.

Pinkney Yes, we do. There's been a bus strike.

Salter Friends. Because we're all friends here. Some of you old friends.

There is banging on the tray from Molly.

Thank you. (*Meaning it to stop here, which it doesn't.*)

Gilchrist That's enough, Molly.

Molly promptly stops.

Salter And if you're seeing this courtesy of *Pennine People*, then you're likely to be a friend, too. One of the many thousands loyal to our much-loved hospital, and who have given us your support. We can all be truly proud of ourselves. I'm afraid, though, that there's no decision yet, so there's still the threat of Tadcaster.

Hazel Where's Tadcaster?

Salter It's not where it is. It's what it is. Big, modern and with a huge catchment area, some people say Tadcaster is the future and that we belong to yesterday already. Well, here at the Beth, cosy, friendly and above all local, we believe that yesterday is the new tomorrow.

Finally, an unexpected pleasure and a great honour for our hospital. Our longest-serving nurse is due to retire in a few weeks' time and, in recognition of her service, the Royal College has awarded her its Bywater Medal, which I am now delighted to present. Sister Gilchrist, our own Lady with the Lamp.

Gilchrist steps up and he pins on the medal.
Some applause, though one call of 'stab her' as he pins it on.
Molly bangs her tray.

Salter That'll do, Mrs Ridsdale.

She continues to bang.

Gilchrist Molly. Knock it off.

She promptly stops.

Salter Sister Gilchrist.

Gilchrist I won't keep you long. Mrs Mathieson wants changing and we're waiting to do the drug round; Miss Proctor's cannula is leaking through its bandage; and I've all the paperwork to do with Mr Colman's unexpected departure this morning. You'll forgive me if I don't gloss

76

over these mundane and possibly distasteful concerns, but they are the small change of a nurse's day. I have switched off my pager, or it would doubtless be reminding me that it's time for Mr Satterthwaite to take his prostate pill, and Mrs Hainsworth her Losec.

Nursing is thought to be a calling. To be a nurse one is expected to have a vocation. My vocation came about like this.

My mother was a widow. I was an only child. When I was thirteen, no older, my mother took to loaning me out, hiring me to be more exact, to anyone who needed help with a senile parent. Typically, it would be someone who said, 'We have to do everything for them.' When anyone says that, as I soon learned, it means they have to do one thing for them . . . clean them up, and this I did. Joyless though my life was, I was still doing it six years later when my mother went the same way and so became what one might call my client, and I her somewhat uncaring carer. Then she died, and I had to find a job.

It was only then that I realised that what I had regarded at best as distasteful and at worst as slavery was in fact my apprenticeship. And so I became a nurse. It was not easy. Nobody had told me that nursing meant passing examinations. Thanks to my mother I had missed much of my schooling so I wasn't much good at that. But I managed the basics, and via a care home graduated to geriatrics, where the finer skills are seldom required. I don't know who the other recipients of the Bywater Medal are, but I imagine they will have credits and diplomas galore. Not me. Because nursing is not my chosen vocation but just where I've landed up though it doesn't make me any less of a nurse . . . as this medal seems to acknowledge . . .

Salter thinks she has finished and gets up.

Salter Thank you . . . sorry!

Gilchrist . . . It has not been easy but all I can say is that I have done what I could.

I shall wear my medal with pride, but it will be a reminder of what nursing used to be like. If I am an award-winner, it is because I am old-fashioned. I have comforted the afflicted. I have treated the sick and I have consoled the dying. Nursing, I have made room.

Salter Thank you, Sister Gilchrist. Outspoken as ever.

The choir sings again.

MUSIC: 'Congratulations' (Cliff Richard).

As they perform, Alex and Cliff are with Salter. They have a laptop. As Salter watches it, cross-fade to:
The camera crew, once more in evidence, this time focusing on Gilchrist. A voice interviewing her, but no light on the interviewer.

Gilchrist Not at all. I was actually looking forward to retirement and hanging up my Marigolds.

When I first started nursing, there was much talk of targets. Targets was the new and exciting idea that was going to galvanise the Health Service. Put in charge of old people, I found it hard to see what targets there could be. And nobody told me.

On any other ward, the target was recovery and discharge. But here if there was recovery there was often no discharge. So there was just one target and that was death.

Voice And you helped them achieve that?

Gilchrist A more rapid turnover on the ward seemed to suit everybody. And I mean everybody.

The doctors, for obvious reasons, the loved ones, so-called, who seldom visited, and when mother or father died, the relatives seemed glad to be relieved of the obligation.

Voice You say everybody seemed pleased. Does that include the patients?

Gilchrist I was a facilitator, self-appointed, I agree, and in any other profession – and nursing is a profession if it is allowed to be – in any other profession, I would be called a progress-chaser.

Voice Did nobody ask?

Gilchrist I am not a doctor. I am a woman. I'm a nurse. Nobody was interested.

Voice Was it just random?

Gilchrist Certainly not, I'm a professional. I didn't just pick on anybody. There had to be a criterion. What makes most work on wards like these is incontinence. I had a list, and as soon as anybody started to soil themselves, they went on it.

Voice Was that where you drew the line? Nobody ever asked?

Gilchrist Not until Mrs Maudsley.

Voice You were fond of Mr Colman?

Gilchrist Well, normally he was clean. I kept a record. I have a notebook somewhere.

Voice Yes. We have it.

Gilchrist I felt I was making a contribution.

Voice By killing old people?

Gilchrist By helping them to die. Clearing the decks.

Voice It's no less murder for being a metaphor.
    You say life was a burden to them. Do you think this is what they would have chosen?

Gilchrist How should they choose between life and death? Most of them can't even choose between mince and macaroni.

Voice We'll take a break there. Interview suspended at 15.35 p.m.

It's only fair to say that you're looking at a very long sentence: life, and with no one to commute it as you so kindly did theirs.

Another interview comes into focus on the other side of the stage: Valentine's hearing.

Voice You're in the news. This nurse. Did you know her?

Valentine Of course.

Voice And you never twigged?

Valentine It's hardly what one expects.

Voice You don't have a suspicious mind. Whereas I do. It's what I'm paid for.

I see you had a student visa but stayed on. Well, at least you didn't come in with a truckload of oranges.

So, what makes you think you would be an asset to this country?

Valentine I am a doctor.

Voice Besides that. We have doctors of our own. You must remember that in England there's not an infinite amount of room. On a Saturday afternoon you can't move, even in Pontefract. Anything else?

Valentine I work with old people.

Voice It's true there's no shortage of those. Mostly white, I take it?

Valentine Why do you say that?

Voice The point I'm making is that being less advanced than we are, you tend to keep your own old people at home. Now, the questions.

I won't insult you by asking who won the 1966 World Cup, but I see that the hospital where you work has a choir.

Valentine It has.

Voice Are you in the choir?

Valentine I sometimes help out.

Voice Well then, you won't mind, just as a formality, if we ask you to sing something. 'Land of Hope and Glory'. Do you want the words?

Valentine No.

Voice That's good.

Valentine (*sings*)
    Land of Hope and Glory,
    Mother of the Free,
    How shall we extol thee,
    Who were born . . .

He stops.

Actually, I can't.

Voice Oh, I was rather enjoying it.

Valentine I've never liked it. Even Elgar hated it.

Voice What's he got to do with it?

Valentine He wrote the music.

Voice But it's not the music you're objecting to, is it? A pity. You were doing so well.

Valentine I'm auditioning to be English. What you're wanting is a Brit.

Voice Good morning, Dr Valentine. Nice try.

Pause.

Oh, and when the time comes, I'd have my bags packed.
They tend to call early in the day.

Colin and Salter watching the titles sequence of the
documentary.
On the monitor: the opening ninety- second title
sequence of their now complete documentary – WHEN
CARERS KILL: DEATH AT THE BETH, *a prime-time*
special. Cut fast, to music with commentary or
captions putting together the highlights of the story:
Salter saying nobody likes old people.
Valentine holding Lucille's hand.
Gilchrist in full kit.
Choir singing, plus the Pudsey Nightingale.
Death of Mrs Maudlsey.
Award of the Bywater Medal.
Salter reading a statement outside the hospital.
Gilchrist escorted to a prison van with screaming
crowd.

Salter You ask me if I knew. I reproach myself now, but
to be honest, I knew and I didn't know, which is often the
case when circumstances not of one's choosing contrive
to work to one's advantage.

Colin I have mixed feelings. I grieve for my father,
naturally. But I'm not sorry about the closure, though it
was none of my doing. And there is a lesson here. It is that
one person with conviction and a degree of self-regard
can even by accident defeat the entirely worthy efforts of
all the rest. Forget the beds trundled up Penyghent, the
urologists abseiling down Gaping Ghyll and the midwives
plunging across Morecambe Bay, all go for nothing when
one person with an agenda of their own wills it otherwise.

Democracy nothing. Will, that is what matters. What carries the day is will.

Salter Yours or hers?

Colin Will and chance. Never mind how many patients she saw off, she certainly killed the hospital.

The patients file on (in their outdoor clothes?) ready to go to Tadcaster, now accompanied by Pinkney, Gerald, Fletcher and Ramesh.

Lucille You've got yourself dolled up.

Mavis Well, we're off to Tadcaster.

Hazel (*pushing Ambrose's wheelchair*) We're looking forward to it, aren't we, Gilbert?

Ambrose 'We', Hazel? 'We'? You and I do not belong together even in the same personal pronoun.

Hazel Well we might at Tadcaster.

Pinkney You won't know you're born. There'll be WiFi, and you'll be able to Skype your loved ones on a daily basis. Skype! Skype!

Neville The other one was a villain. Now this one's taken leave of her senses.

Pinkney Trust me. Tadcaster will be heaven. (*To Ramesh and Fletcher.*) Are you coming?

Ramesh No.

Fletcher No fear. There's a posh clinic just starting.

Pinkney Where?

Ramesh The in-place.

Pinkney Dubai?

Fletcher *Hull!*

Mary Tadcaster's a bit far for folks to come, visitors.

Cora Well they never do come.

Mary Yes, only now they'll have an excuse.

Ambrose Are you not coming?

Valentine To Tadcaster? I'm not asked. Having presented my furtive self for examination and been found wanting, I shan't be available. Besides, I've been told I'm too hands-on.

He takes Ambrose's hand.

Ambrose I shall miss you. You've saved my life.

Valentine No.

Ambrose No. You're right. Nobody saves anyone's life. Just postpones their death.

Valentine That's the spirit.

Valentine pats him reassuringly.

Valentine He'll come.

Ambrose Oh yes. In some shape or form.

Valentine turns front.

Valentine Nurse Pinkney was right when she said Tadcaster was going to be heaven. Only she never got to be an angel there, a casualty of the downsizing that privatisation inevitably involves.

Still, with the nurses largely from the Philippines, where they are brought up to treat the old with more respect, there were no complaints from the patients.

Who now go off, singing.

MUSIC: 'Side by Side' (Dean Martin).

Salter and Colin in separate spots.

Salter Though I managed to snap up the hospital buildings for one of my property companies, I was hoping for some appropriate recognition of my services in the form of a knighthood. Thanks to Sister Gilchrist, all I've ended up with is a measly CBE. However, after some well-placed philanthropy, at our local university I managed my heart's desire in the form of an honorary degree. So now I am at last Doctor Salter.

And perhaps we see him in his academic robes.

Colin Salter notwithstanding, the sale represents a healthy capital gain for NHS funding, the hospital having reinvented itself as a boutique hotel, with, in a graceful acknowledgement of its previous existence, the principal suites named after Florence Nightingale and Edith Cavell. For the moment, its best-known nurse remains uncommemorated, though a play about her is threatened at the local theatre.

Valentine I see Alma, as I'm now permitted to call her, from time to time. It's a place in the wilds of Lincolnshire.

In the prison garden.

Gilchrist I'm not unhappy.

I share a garden which I've never had. I prefer plants that grow in the shade. And I paint. All that. I'm still a celebrity only it's wearing off. I don't imagine I will ever be released. Though in case it would help I was advised to say sorry. Show some remorse.

Valentine And did you?

Gilchrist I did . . . but no one believes me.

And they're quite right . . . I took . . . a short cut . . . several . . . I can see that. But if people love their parents why do they put them away?

Valentine Are you asking me?

Gilchrist No. That's what I asked them. They said it wasn't remorse.

Only it's honest.

She takes his hand.

Will you come again?

Valentine How can I? I am forbidden these shores.

Gilchrist Will you write?

Valentine (*turning out front*) It was a difficult conversation and in one of the many pauses, for want of anything better, I said –

(*Turning back to her*) When I was doing my training, before I plumped for geriatrics, I was very keen on surgery. Through observing and even participating in colorectal surgery, I was struck by something extraordinary, namely that the flesh of the bowel of mature and even aged patients was no different from that of the flesh of a child or a young person. Unique among every department of the body, the bowel does not seem to age. So these ancient and faltering persons, carry within their venerable bodies a remnant of their infant selves, part of them still young and ageless.

Why? Solve that and you would undoubtedly get the Nobel Prize.

So you see, Alma, nobody can be quite written off, even the Pudsey Nightingale.

Gilchrist Perhaps.

She continues to garden. Valentine turns front again.

Valentine Well, at least she has her place, even if that place is prison. Me, I have no place.

Come unto these yellow sands and there take hands. Only not mine, and so, unwelcome on these grudging shores, I must leave the burden of being English to others and become what I have always felt, a displaced person.

86

Why, I ask myself, should I still want to join? What is there for me here, where education is a privilege and nationality a boast? Starving the sick and neglecting the old, what makes you special still? There is nobody to touch you, but who wants to any more? Open your arms before it's too late.

In the meantime, though I cannot be English, I remain a doctor, if only in places where nobody asks questions . . . a doctor on a cruise ship for instance where, who knows, I might even meet somebody and have a shipboard romance.

So when you next go on a cruise to the Adriatic or the Greek Islands and get that nasty tummy bug, take another look at the ship's doctor.

It might be me.

He smiles.